Invitation to Matthew

This volume continues a new series of commentaries specially designed to answer the need for a lively, contemporary guide to the written Word. Here is the best of contemporary biblical scholarship, together with the world-renowned Jerusalem Bible text. In addition, there are study questions that will provoke and inspire further discussion.

The Gospel of Matthew was written for a segment of the early church that desperately needed a sense of identity with the past and some direction for facing an uncertain future. The Christians of that time still had their roots in Judaism, but a revolt against Rome, which had caused the destruction of the temple at Jerusalem, made the Jewish people more suspicious of Christians than they had been previously. It was indeed a moment of religious crisis for Matthew's church. What had happened to the sense of kinship with the past? Was it right to launch into a strange and untracked future? To this church, Matthew wrote of a Jesus whose origins went back deep into the history of Israel, a Jesus who was the Messiah promised by God.

How very much like Matthew's church is the post-conciliar church of our day. And how very much, too, does the modern believer need the reassurance of traditional ties. A close study of Matthew's Gospel reminds the faithful that we are members of the same church, whose roots both past and present rest in Christ.

INVITATION TO MATTHEW presents the Gospel and its message in a format that can be easily used for individual study, daily meditation, and/or group discussion. In short, it is an indispensable volume for any Christian library.

INVITATION TO MATTHEW

INVITATION
TO MATTHEW

*A Commentary on the Gospel of Matthew with
Complete Text from The Jerusalem Bible*

DONALD SENIOR

IMAGE BOOKS
A Division of Doubleday & Company, Inc.
Garden City, New York
1977

ISBN: 0-385-12211-x
Library of Congress Catalog Card Number 77–73337

CONTENTS

THE BOOKS OF
THE BIBLE ABBREVIATIONS

Ac	Acts	Lk	Luke
Am	Amos	Lm	Lamentations
Ba	Baruch	Lv	Leviticus
1 Ch	1 Chronicles	1 M	1 Maccabees
2 Ch	2 Chronicles	2 M	2 Maccabees
1 Co	2 Corinthians	Mi	Micah
2 Co	2 Corinthians	Mk	Mark
Col	Colossians	Ml	Malachi
Dn	Daniel	Mt	Matthew
Dt	Deuteronomy	Na	Nahum
Ep	Ephesians	Nb	Numbers
Est	Esther	Ne	Nehemiah
Ex	Exodus	Ob	Obadiah
Ezk	Ezekiel	1 P	1 Peter
Ezr	Ezra	2 P	2 Peter
Ga	Galatians	Ph	Philippians
Gn	Genesis	Phm	Philemon
Hab	Habakkuk	Pr	Proverbs
Heb	Hebrews	Ps	Psalms
Hg	Haggai	Qo	Ecclesiastes
Ho	Hosea	Rm	Romans
Is	Isaiah	Rt	Ruth
Jb	Job	Rv	Revelation
Jdt	Judith	1 S	1 Samuel
Jg	Judges	2 S	2 Samuel
Jl	Joel	Sg	Song of Songs
Jm	James	Si	Ecclesiasticus
Jn	John	Tb	Tobit
1 Jn	1 John	1 Th	1 Thessalonians
2 Jn	2 John	2 Th	2 Thessalonians
3 Jn	3 John	1 Tm	1 Timothy
Jon	Jonah	2 Tm	2 Timothy
Jos	Joshua	Tt	Titus
Jr	Jeremiah	Ws	Wisdom
Jude	Jude	Zc	Zechariah
1 K	1 Kings	Zp	Zephaniah
2 K	2 Kings		

GENERAL INTRODUCTION TO
THE DOUBLEDAY NEW TESTAMENT
COMMENTARY SERIES*

Let me introduce this new commentary series on the New Testament by sharing some experiences. In my job as New Testament Book Review Editor for the *Catholic Biblical Quarterly,* scores of books pass through my hands each year. As I evaluate these books and send them out to reviewers, I cannot help but think that so little of this scholarly research will make its way into the hands of the educated lay person.

In talking at biblical institutes and to charismatic and lay study groups, I find an almost unquenchable thirst for the Word of God. People want to learn more; they want to study. But when they ask me to recommend commentaries on the New Testament, I'm stumped. What commentaries can I put into their hands, commentaries that do not have the technical jargon of scholars and that really communicate to the educated lay person?

The goal of this commentary series is to make the best of contemporary scholarship available to the educated lay person in a highly readable and understandable way. The commentaries avoid footnotes and other scholarly apparatus. They are short and sweet. The authors make their points in a clear way and don't fatigue their readers with unnecessary detail.

Another outstanding feature of this commentary series is that it is based on the Jerusalem Bible translation, which is serialized with the commentary. This lively and easily understandable translation has received rave reviews from millions of readers. It is the interstate of translations and avoids the stop lights of local-road translations.

A signal feature of the commentaries on the Gospels is that they explore the way each evangelist used the sayings and deeds of Jesus to meet the needs of his church. The commentators answer the question: How did each evangelist guide, challenge, teach, and console the members of his community with the message of Jesus? The commentators are not interested in the evangelist's message for its own sake, but explain that message with one eye on present application.

This last-mentioned feature goes hand and glove with the innovative feature of appending Study Questions to the explanations of individual passages. By means of these Study Questions, the commentator moves from an explanation of the message of the evangelist to a consideration of how this message might apply to believers today.

Each commentator has two highly important qualifications: scholarly expertise and the proven ability to communicate the results of solid scholarship to the people of God.

I am confident that this new commentary series will meet a real need as it helps people to unlock a door to the storehouse of God's Word, where they will find food for life.

ROBERT J. KARRIS, O.F.M.
Associate Professor of New Testament Studies,
Catholic Theological Union and
Chicago Cluster of Theological Schools

INTRODUCTION

Few Christians turn to the Gospels to brush up on their history or to solve theoretical problems. The believer seeks out the Gospels for inspiration and life. This instinctive estimate of the Gospels' purpose is corroborated by the results of modern biblical studies. The Gospels were not written to fill out Jesus' biographical dossier, nor are they abstract religious treatises. Each of the Gospels summons up an image of Jesus and his meaning for life designed to respond to the religious hopes and agonies of a specific community of Christians. The Gospels, like an effective sermon, tailor their message to a particular audience and a particular mood.

Matthew wrote his Gospel for a segment of the early church that desperately needed a sense of identity with the past and some direction for facing an uncertain future. The original recipients of the Gospel were, as far as can be detected, mainly Jewish Christians, probably living in Syria in the decade between A.D. 80 and 90.

The time and the place are significant. It was a time when those Christians whose roots were still in Judaism and its sacred history experienced the agony of a wrenching separation, even alienation, from the religion of their fathers. Prior to the Jewish revolt against Rome in A.D. 66, Judaism and Christianity seem to have maintained relatively peaceful, if not cordial, relationships. The book of Acts testifies that Palestinian Christians continued to worship in the Jerusalem Temple (Acts 2:46), and the ranks of the young church were swelled by an influx of Pharisees as well as Samaritans and Greek-speaking Jews. The early Christians considered themselves to be thoroughly in tune with the religious history of Israel; they were the people of the renewed covenant, of the Messianic age so longed for by the Hebrew Scriptures. At the same time, those Jews who rejected the claims of Jesus and his followers could still maintain enough tolerance for such fringe groups as the Christians seemed to be. There were local harassments and some degree of hostility and debate, but, in general, Jews who were Christians and Jews who were not seemed able to share a live-and-let-live attitude.

But as history moved to the decade of Matthew, A.D. 80–90, some enormous changes engulfed both Judaism and Christianity and led to the crisis atmosphere that helped trigger Matthew's Gospel. A key event for both religious traditions was Rome's suppression of the Jewish revolt of A.D. 66–73. When the armies of the Roman general Titus pulverized the last fragments of resistance in Jerusalem and destroyed the sacred city and its still more sacred Temple, in A.D. 70, the destinies of both Jews and Christians were profoundly altered.

For Judaism it meant the end of an era. The Temple, which had been the unifying religious symbol of Israel, was gone and so was the effective influence of such groups as the priests and the Sadducees, who had been a major part of the nation's leadership. Gone, too, were the Zealots, who had precipitated the revolt, and reform groups such as the Essenes. The only party resilient enough and astute enough to survive the war was the Pharisees. Under the leadership of Yoḥanan ben Zakkai, the sages of the Pharisee party gathered at the coastal town of Jamnia and began to blueprint an orthodox Judaism without temple or priesthood. Now the local synagogue, with its emphasis on the teaching of the Scriptures, would be the focal point of Jewish identity. Israel's worship of Yahweh would not be the ancient ritual of Temple sacrifice but the "holocaust" of strict obedience to the Law, the Law interpreted and taught by the rabbis. The moral strength and leadership of the Pharisees enabled Judaism to survive one of the most violent shocks of its long and often tragic history. But, perhaps of necessity, it also meant an end to much of the tolerance for religious diversity that had characterized pre-70 Judaism. The increasing strength of Christianity and its claim to be the inheritor of the promises of the Hebrew Scriptures would lead to a sharp and often bitter cleavage between what were now seen clearly as two distinct religious entities.

The destruction of Jerusalem and its Temple also effected fundamental changes on early Christianity. Prior to A.D. 70, the religious center of Christianity had remained Jerusalem and the Jewish Christian leaders. But the sacking of Jerusalem put an effective end to this center of influence in the early church. For years prior to 70, gentiles had been streaming into the community; now they would be the dominant voice and culture in the young church. Christianity had accelerated its move to the west. As it did so, its distinction from Judaism would become more apparent and its debates with the Jewish leaders more heated.

Some sense of this complex history of the first century is necessary in order to fully appreciate Matthew's Gospel. For it is in response to this situation that the evangelist wrote his Gospel. The Christians of

Matthew's community were witnesses to these turbulent years of transition and disruption. Most of them were Jews who had come to accept Jesus as the Messiah and Son of God. And they had seen their community grow with increasing numbers of new converts, Greeks and other gentiles from the mixed population centers of Syria. Their acceptance of Jesus had never meant for them a repudiation of their Jewish past. Jesus was the Christ, the fulfillment of Israel's dream.

But now this continuity with their sacred past seemed threatened with rupture. Gentile converts brought strange customs, many of which contravened the Jewish Law and were repugnant to refined Jewish moral sensitivities. And with the destruction of Jerusalem and the reorganization at Jamnia, these Jewish Christians had to contend with the hostility of their fellow Jews. They were accused of destroying the Law and of forfeiting their claim on the Jewish Scriptures. They were not to be part of the destiny of Israel promised by God, and they were banned from participation in Jewish synagogues.

It was a moment of religious crisis for Matthew's church. What had happened to one's sense of kinship with the past? Was it right to launch into a strange and untracked future? Matthew's church was infected with the perennial virus of people in transition: loss of perspective and disunity. This was the pastoral situation to which Matthew's Gospel attempted to respond. By editing the already written Gospel of Mark, by including precious materials about Jesus found in a collection of his sayings, and by incorporating a number of traditions known to Matthew and his community, the evangelist would shape a story of Jesus' life that would have special meaning for his distraught Christians. The details of Matthew's pointed story will be spun out in the text and commentary that follow. For the moment, we can simply alert the reader to some of Matthew's story-telling lore.

The framework of Matthew's message encompasses a full story of the life of Jesus. (I) Matthew's distinctive recital of this story begins with the remote origins of Jesus in the history of Israel and with the portent-laden traditions about his infancy (Chs. 1–2). These events and the epic meeting of John the Baptist and Jesus (3:1 to 4:11) orientate the reader to the dramatic beginning of Jesus' ministry as the Messiah. (II) The story quickens with Jesus' entry into Galilee. In this first great section of the public history of Jesus (4:12 to 10:42), Matthew will portray Jesus as the fulfillment of Israel's hope, as the Messiah who comes to teach genuine wisdom (Chs. 5–7) and to bring deep healing (8–9) to God's people. His ministry of restoring life to Israel is one that is shared with his disciples and those who will take their place (9:3 to 10:42). (III) Another phase of the Gospel begins in Chapter 11 (11:1 to 16:20). The mood runs sober as Matthew charts the varying responses to Jesus and his message. Jesus, like John, will be rejected by his own people. That rejection leads to the climax of Jesus' ministry in Jerusalem. (IV) Matthew begins to orientate the reader toward that fateful conclusion in a central section of the Gospel that opens (16:21) with the first Passion prediction and carries to the end of Chapter 20, in which Jesus and his frightened disciples stand before the capital city. (V) The most dramatic moments of Jesus' saga take place in the City of the Prophets (21:1 to 28:15). Here Matthew will recount Jesus' forceful presence in the Temple, his last teach-

ing, and the measured recital of his suffering and
death. Jerusalem will also be the locale for the startling
events that demonstrate that Jesus' death was no mere
tragedy but a pivotal event in the history of the world.
Matthew closes his story back in Galilee (28:16–20).
A new community born out of Jesus' resurrection is
sent out on a world-wide mission.

This story line carries Matthew's Gospel from start
to finish. But one of the distinctive elements of this
Gospel is its concentration on the *words* of Jesus.
Throughout the history of Jesus, Matthew will freeze
the pace of the Gospel to include collections of the
words of Jesus or "discourses" (cf. the Sermon on the
Mount of Chapters 5–7, the mission discourse of
Chapter 10, the parable discourse of Chapter 13, the
community discourse of Chapter 18, and the judgment
discourse of Chapters 23–25). Matthew's use of so
many sayings and parables of Jesus heightens his portrayal of Jesus as teacher, as one who reveals true wisdom to God's people.

By means of this narrative and its majestic portrait
of Jesus, Matthew attempts to respond to the needs of
his community. The very choice of this medium points
to the dominant motif of Matthew's pastoral strategy.
It is faith in Jesus Christ and a genuine commitment to
his message that will give perspective to Matthew's
suffering church. The reader of the Gospel should be
alerted to some of the ways in which the evangelist
goes about his task:

1. He portrays *Jesus as the embodiment and
fulfillment of all that Israel hoped for*. Matthew depicts
Jesus as showing marked respect for the Law, for Israel's institutions, and even for the leaders who ultimately oppose him (23:2–3). Jesus has come not to

destroy but to fulfill (5:17–20). He is *the* Israelite, the obedient Son of Yahweh. This is a case Matthew will build steadily throughout his narrative and over which he frequently lingers by explicit references to the Old Testament Scriptures (cf. an explanation of the so-called "fulfillment" quotations in the commentary on 1:22).

By stressing Jesus as the fulfillment of Israel, Matthew reminds his Christians that in following Jesus they are not abandoning their heritage but discovering its full meaning.

2. Matthew also interprets *the events of Jesus' life, particularly his death and resurrection, as the pivotal events in salvation history.* Jesus' roots go back to Abraham and David. He is the promised Messiah. And in accord with God's promises, he comes first to Israel (10:5; 15:24). The tragic rejection of Jesus becomes a paradox of providence because God's plan of salvation will not be thwarted, even by Israel's infidelity. Now the invitation to the banquet of the kingdom is thrown open to the gentiles. Thus the death and resurrection of Jesus begin a new and final age, an age in which the good news of the kingdom will be brought to the whole world, and an age in which the old order of the Mosaic Law would be completed and replaced by the teaching of Jesus.

By viewing history through the lens of the Gospel, Matthew wanted to give his baffled Christians perspective on the disturbing changes they were experiencing and to counter the accusations coming from the synagogue. As Matthew stresses in his infancy narrative, the God of Israel had consistently used the unexpected and unassuming as instruments of his providence. The flood of gentiles into God's vineyard was another of those marvelous surprises tucked into sacred history. One had to be open and ready for God's will.

3. And finally, Matthew sees *Jesus as a model of the inner life of the community* as it moves into its future. Jesus' teaching on love and reconciliation, his ministry of compassion, and above all, his life-giving death, challenge the community to mold its own priorities on those of Jesus. Matthew's Christ is a *doer* who constantly scores the hypocrisy of words uncoupled from deeds. The Gospel's robust and even angry critique of the opponents of Jesus makes them a vivid example of what the Christian ought *not* to be: insensitive legalists, blind leaders, and teachers who do not follow their own words.

Here again Matthew's ministry of continuity, of perspective, is at work. For through the teaching and example of Jesus, he reminds his community that the only link with the past worth saving was Israel's call to fidelity. Obedience to the will of the Father was always the mark of a true Israelite, and that was the mark of Jesus and those who were his followers.

Matthew's church is a long distance from our own. Even though we know something about the agony of transition and discontinuity, the particular turbulence of the infant church in first-century Syria is not the kind we experience. But this does not make Matthew's Gospel a relic. Crisis has always triggered the best in Christian reflection. The experience of change, of suffering, of hopes uncertain, can force us to dig deep into our tradition and to discover its power anew. So Matthew and his church must have done. His Gospel is "gospel" because it represents a Spirit-filled portrait of Jesus and his significance that is no longer local but universal, able to be "Good News" for all those who believe in Jesus and hope to find perspective in him. It is the intention of the comments that follow to catch some of the beauty and power of Matthew's message.

As my work on this book is completed, I want to thank Miriam Senior for helping me with the manuscript and Sr. Patricia Mattox for patiently typing it. The book is dedicated to my students at Catholic Theological Union. They keep reminding me that a Gospel is for life, and for that I am grateful.

DONALD SENIOR, C.P.
January 20, 1977

Prologue
The Gospel Begins to Break into the World
Matthew 1:1 to 4:16

Matthew 1:1–17
JESUS' FAMILY TREE

1 **1** A genealogy of Jesus Christ, son of David, son of Abraham:

2 Abraham was the father of Isaac,
Isaac the father of Jacob,
Jacob the father of Judah and his brothers,

3 Judah was the father of Perez and Zerah,
  Tamar being their mother,
Perez was the father of Hezron,
Hezron was the father of Ram,

4 Ram was the father of Amminadab,
Amminadab the father of Nahshon,
Nahshon the father of Salmon,

5 Salmon was the father of Boaz, Rahab being
  his mother,
Boaz was the father of Obed, Ruth being his
  mother,
Obed was the father of Jesse;

6 and Jesse was the father of King David.

David was the father of Solomon, whose
  mother had been Uriah's wife,

7 Solomon was the father of Rehoboam,
Rehoboam the father of Abijah,
Abijah the father of Asa,

8 Asa was the father of Jehoshaphat,
Jehoshaphat the father of Joram,
Joram the father of Azariah,

9   Azariah was the father of Jotham,
     Jotham the father of Ahaz,
     Ahaz the father of Hezekiah,
10   Hezekiah was the father of Manasseh,
     Manasseh the father of Amon,
     Amon the father of Josiah;
11   and Josiah was the father of Jechoniah and his
         brothers.
     Then the deportation to Babylon took place.

12   After the deportation to Babylon:
     Jechoniah was the father of Shealtiel,
     Shealtiel the father of Zerubbabel,
13   Zerubbabel was the father of Abiud,
     Abiud the father of Eliakim,
     Eliakim the father of Azor,

14   Azor was the father of Zadok,
     Zadok the father of Achim,
     Achim the father of Eliud,
15   Eliud was the father of Eleazar,
     Eleazar the father of Matthan,
     Matthan the father of Jacob;
16   and Jacob was the father of Joseph the husband
         of Mary;
     of her was born Jesus who is called Christ.
17   The sum of generations is therefore: fourteen
     from Abraham to David; fourteen from David
     to the Babylonian deportation; and fourteen from
     the Babylonian deportation to Christ.

✠

The series of brief and colorful events that precede
the beginning of Jesus' public ministry serve as a prologue to Matthew's Gospel. The first two chapters,
which recount the story of Jesus' infancy, begin
Matthew's "ministry of continuity" (cf. the Introduction): carefully making his case that Jesus is fully,
faithfully Jewish, a Son of his Father, a model of

fidelity, the very embodiment of Yahweh's presence among his people. The prologue also begins to highlight those aspects of the gospel message that Matthew favors: a paradoxical sensitivity to things Jewish and to universalism, a close attention to the way people respond to Jesus and his message.

"A genealogy of Jesus Christ, son of David, son of Abraham." These opening words serve as a title page for the prologue and seem to subtly hint at the entire span of the Gospel story. "Genealogy" translates the Greek term *genesis,* or literally, "origin." Matthew's opening phrase echoes Genesis 2:4 and 5:1, where the Bible speaks of the creation of the universe and the story of the descendants of Adam. By using this phrase, the evangelist hints that what will follow is not the account of an ordinary family tree but the origin of one whose place in world history is cosmic and unparalleled.

The titles given to Jesus in this opening verse have been strategically chosen. He is the "Christ, son of David" (cf. 1 S 8), thus the promised redeemer and king who would fulfill Israel's centuries of yearning for justice, peace, and freedom. He is "son of Abraham." Jesus' Jewish roots sink deeper yet, back to the Patriarch, whose trusting pilgrimage from Ur had begun the long history of God's people (Gn 12).

The reference to Abraham is also the first of many signals that the final destiny of God's people would be more than they expected. As the New Testament writers were quick to note, Abraham predated the covenant and the Law. He was, in a sense, the father of all nations (Gn 12:2–3), a solitary figure whose fidelity showed that ultimately it was not membership in a par-

ticular race or caste that made one righteous but one's
integrity before God.

This dual track—firmly and faithfully Jewish and
unexpectedly universal—leaves its mark on the carefully designed list of names that spans the generations
from Abraham to Jesus. The casual reader might consider this genealogical table a boring bit of obscure history, but tucked within these verses are important
themes of Matthew's Gospel. Its function is not to provide clinching historical information. The list of names
is partially borrowed from the long genealogical table
of the First Book of Chronicles but has been edited
and clipped to fit the Gospel's purpose. That purpose is
less archival than theological, it is a statement about
Jesus' continuity with the past. His family history is
bound up with those multiple generations of Jews who
kept God's promise alive from the beginning with the
Patriarch Abraham to the glory of David and the Jewish kings, through the wracking experience of exile,
and down to the moment of Jesus' own entry into history.

However, the measured cadences of this genealogical
list and its numerical symmetry (cf. v. 17) belie the
note of the "unexpected," of *discontinuity*, which
Matthew also subtly includes. In verses 3, 5, and 6 the
names of four women break the rhythm of the list:
Tamar, Rahab, Ruth, Bathsheba (referred to as
"Uriah's wife"). These, plus Mary, Jesus' mother, are
the only women mentioned in the genealogy, and each
of them has a rather unusual niche in Jewish history:
Tamar, the Canaanite woman who seduced her father-
in-law, Judah (Gn 38); Rahab, the prostitute of Jericho who aided the Israelite spies and helped insure the
conquest of the promised land (Jos 2:1–21); Ruth,

the Moabite who with the help of Naomi snares Boaz as her husband (Rt); Bathsheba, the wife of a Hittite and the mother of Solomon, whose beauty kindles lust and murder in King David (2 S 11:2).

Some commentators speculate that these women are listed to offset hostile rumors about the circumstances of Jesus' own birth. But Matthew's purpose seems to be deeper than mere defense. Each of these women were admired as heroines in Jewish folklore because of their astuteness and resourcefulness. And each of them is a foreigner who breaks completely unexpectedly into Jewish history and even into the lineage of the Messiah.

Thus Matthew, by reminding his readers of the extraordinary ways God has acted in the past, may intend not only to blunt hostile innuendos against the tradition of Jesus' virginal conception (a tradition strongly affirmed by Matthew in 1:18–25) but also to send up another signal about the "outsiders." It had happened in Israel's past: God had incorporated non-Jews into the history of his people. Through the power of God's Spirit, it could happen again.

STUDY QUESTION: The Gospel detects God at work in history, often in unexpected ways. Are we able to discover this same power in our own lives?

Matthew 1:18–25
NAMING GOD'S SON

¹⁸ This is how Jesus Christ came to be born. His mother Mary was betrothed to Joseph; but before they came to live together she was found to ¹⁹ be with child through the Holy Spirit. ·Her husband Joseph, being a man of honor and wanting to spare her publicity, decided to divorce ²⁰ her informally. ·He had made up his mind to do this when the angel of the Lord appeared to him in a dream and said, "Joseph son of David, do not be afraid to take Mary home as your wife, because she has conceived what is in her by the ²¹ Holy Spirit. ·She will give birth to a son and you must name him Jesus, because he is the one ²² who is to save his people from their sins." ·Now all this took place to fulfill the words spoken by the Lord through the prophet:

²³ The virgin will conceive and give birth to a son
   and they will call him Immanuel,

²⁴ a name which means "God-is-with-us." ·When Joseph woke up he did what the angel of the Lord had told him to do: he took his wife to his ²⁵ home ·and, though he had not had intercourse with her, she gave birth to a son; and he named him Jesus.

✠

The Gospel now focuses on the most important phase of the long genealogy, the birth of Jesus. Matthew is not concerned with picturesque details. The moment of birth itself is somewhat prosaically noted in verse 25. Instead, the evangelist stressed the divine origin of Jesus and, above all, his significance.

The narrative introduces us to Joseph, the husband of Mary and the hero of Matthew's infancy story. Joseph's Davidic bloodline makes Jesus legally a part of the royal family (16), and by carying out God's guiding commands Joseph protects Jesus for his future work. Joseph's description as a just man (19), his many dreams (1:20; 2:13, 19), and his eventual forced journey to Egypt (2:14), suggest that the evangelist may be subtly casting Mary's husband along the lines of another famous Joseph, the Old Testament patriarch who played such a key role in the history of Israel (Gn 37–50).

When betrothed to Mary, Joseph discovers that she is with child. The Gospel immediately informs the reader of Jesus' divine origin: Mary is with child "through the Holy Spirit" (18). But Joseph will learn of this only later. He is a "man of honor" (literally, a "just" man), a quality that seems to stress his compassion for Mary, because he decided to waive his right (Dt 24:1) to bring public charges against her.

The angel's message to Joseph brings us to the climax of Matthew's opening chapter. The mission of God's Son is revealed in the names he is given. He is to be called "Jesus," literally "Yahweh is salvation." Matthew will repeat this name in his Gospel more than any other evangelist. The angel stresses its significance: "he is . . . to *save* his people from their sins" (21). The entire Gospel flashes by at this moment: Jesus' words of compassion and forgiveness, his miraculous healings and exorcisms, his graceful and wise teaching, above all his death, which Matthew will call a covenant in blood "for the forgiveness of sins" (26:28).

The evangelist himself breaks into the narrative in verse 22, and introduces a style of Old Testament quotation that will be a special feature of his Gospel. Twelve times, Matthew applies an Old Testament citation to a specific incident of Jesus' life with an introductory formula practically identical to the one in verse 22: "this took place to fulfill the words spoken by the Lord through the prophet. . . ." These quotations illustrate the Gospel's deep conviction that every detail of Jesus' life fulfills the dreams and promises of the Old Testament (cf. 5:17–20).

The Gospel's first fulfillment quotation is one of its most striking. Jesus' entry into human history fulfills the promise of Isaiah 7:14, "the maiden is with child and will soon give birth to a son whom she will call Immanuel." The original quotation was a promise of God relayed to King Ahaz by Isaiah. If the king's faith were strong enough, he would see that God's power would insure the people's survival. The new life begun in the womb of a young Jewish maiden was a precious sign of this promise, a promise revealed in the name he was to bear, "Immanuel," God-with-us. Judaism understood that this promise would be fulfilled in the coming of the Messiah. For Matthew and his community, the words of Isaiah perfectly describe the identity of Jesus and the significance of his birth. They serve as

testimony to the virginal conception of Jesus and
thereby underline God's saving initiative in gifting creation with its most beautiful moment. And the name
"Immanuel" reveals a further dimension of Jesus' mission. He will save the people because he is "God-with-
us." Jesus, God's Son, is Immanuel because he will reveal the Father's will and establish his kingdom. The
very shape of the title, "God-with-us," evokes the
image of the covenant forged between Yahweh and Israel. Jesus is the embodiment of that covenant and its
definitive renewal. The promise of abiding presence
that begins Matthew's Gospel will be matched by the
promise that ends it: "and know that *I am with you* always; yes, to the end of time" (28:20).

STUDY QUESTION: The Gospel lavishes powerful
names on Jesus: "Savior," "God-
with-us." Do these names make
sense to us? Do they express the
meaning Jesus has for our lives?

Matthew 2:1–12
FIRST REACTIONS TO JESUS

1 2 After Jesus had been born at Bethlehem in
Judaea during the reign of King Herod, some
wise men came to Jerusalem from the east.
2 "Where is the infant king of the Jews?" they
asked. "We saw his star as it rose and have come
3 to do him homage." ·When King Herod heard
this he was perturbed, and so was the whole of
4 Jerusalem. ·He called together all the chief priests
and the scribes of the people, and inquired of
5 them where the Christ was to be born. ·"At
Bethlehem in Judaea," they told him, "for this
is what the prophet wrote:

6   And you, Bethlehem, in the land of Judah,
     you are by no means least among the leaders of
        Judah,
     for out of you will come a leader
     who will shepherd my people Israels."

7 Then Herod summoned the wise men to see him
privately. He asked them the exact date on which
8 the star had appeared, ·and sent them on to
Bethlehem. "Go and find out all about the child,"
he said, "and when you have found him, let me
know, so that I too may go and do him homage."
9 Having listened to what the king had to say, they
set out. And there in front of them was the star
they had seen rising; it went forward and halted
10 over the place where the child was. ·The sight

11 of the star filled them with delight, •and going
into the house they saw the child with his mother
Mary, and falling to their knees they did him
homage. Then, opening their treasures, they
offered him gifts of gold and frankincense and
12 myrrh. •But they were warned in a dream not
to go back to Herod, and returned to their own
country by a different way.

☩

Matthew's Gospel is especially concerned with *response* to Jesus and his message. This aspect of the Gospel will begin to be played out in the second chapter of Matthew's infancy narrative.

In this section of the Gospel, the reader will encounter a special type of literary technique. The stories about Herod and the wise men, and about Jesus' journey from Bethlehem to Nazareth by way of Egypt, weave together Old Testament quotations, popular Jewish stories about Old Testament heroes, and basic elements of the gospel tradition about Jesus into a rich and complex literary tapestry. The technique is reminiscent of an ancient Jewish literary craft called "midrash," which was an artful combination of scriptural interpretation and reflection on contemporary events.

The story of Herod and the wise men contrasts the attitudes of two different groups of Jesus' contemporaries, one a faithless king and his Jerusalem court, the other, sincere searchers for the truth who come from afar.

Herod, the clever and ruthless Idumean who became king of Israel under Roman auspices, is joined by "the whole of Jerusalem" (3) in his disturbance at the news that an infant king of the Jews is born. He has at his

disposal the Scriptures and learned men to interpret
them (4–5). Although they correctly deduce that the
Messiah is to be born in Bethlehem (cf. the quotation
from Micah 5:1 which Matthew alters to read "by *no
means* least" instead of the original "the least," thereby
emphasizing the greatness that the birth of Jesus brings
to this insignificant Judean village), the Jewish leaders
begin to plot against Jesus' life. The first note of the
Passion story has already tolled.

The wise men, gentile astrologists from the east, are
guided only by a mysterious star (see below). Their
careful scrutiny of nature has led them to the threshold
of belief. The information they seek from the Jews and
their Scriptures, and God's own guidance, lead them to
Bethlehem, where they are the first to pay Jesus the
real homage he deserves (10–11). The gospel's rejection by Israel, and its acceptance by gentiles, have already been previewed in this opening chapter of the
Messiah's life.

This clever story of a ruler's hostility, of honorable
foreigners, of a guiding star, and of God's providence
tips us off to the Old Testament tradition that provides
the backdrop for this section of the Gospel. The Book
of Numbers (Chs. 22–24) narrates a curious event
during the Exodus. Moses is threatened by the evil
King Balak, who calls on the services of a foreign sor-
cerer, Balaam "from the East" (Nb 23:7). But
Balaam refuses to deliver a curse, as Balak desired,
and instead pronounces a prophetic blessing over
Moses and the people, a blessing that predicts a great
future for Israel and the emergence of a Messianic
king. The blessing includes these words, which surely
influenced the story of the Magi: "I see him—but not
in the present, I behold him—but not close at hand: a

star from Jacob takes the leadership, a sceptre arises from Israel" (Nb 24:17). Later Jewish tradition understood the "star" to be a reference to the Messiah.

This Old Testament tradition beneath the surface of the Magi story allows the evangelist to transmit an almost subliminal message which helps interpret the history of Jesus. Herod is another Balak, who will vainly try to stop God's salvific power. Jesus is a new Moses who will lead his people to freedom. The wise men, like Balaam, testify to the incredible vitality of God's providence. The Exodus could not be thwarted; neither will the Gospel.

STUDY QUESTION: The wise men's search for truth and the blindness of Israel's leaders are the first of many sober warnings in Matthew's Gospel. The outsider's sincerity can often be a jolting challenge to those within the warm confines of established churches.

Matthew 2:13–23
YOU CAN'T GO HOME AGAIN
THE BEGINNING OF THE GOSPEL
PILGRIMAGE

13 After they had left, the angel of the Lord appeared to Joseph in a dream and said, "Get up, take the child and his mother with you, and escape into Egypt, and stay there until I tell you, because Herod intends to search for the child 14 and do away with him." ·So Joseph got up and, taking the child and his mother with him, left 15 that night for Egypt, ·where he stayed until Herod was dead. This was to fulfill what the Lord had spoken through the prophet:

I called my son out of Egypt.

16 Herod was furious when he realized that he had been outwitted by the wise men, and in Bethlehem and its surrounding district he had all the male children killed who were two years old or under, reckoning by the date he had been 17 careful to ask the wise men. ·It was then that the words spoken through the prophet Jeremiah were fulfilled:

18   A voice was heard in Ramah,
     sobbing and loudly lamenting:
     it was Rachel weeping for her children,

> refusing to be comforted
> because they were no more.

19 After Herod's death, the angel of the Lord
20 appeared in a dream to Joseph in Egypt ·and
said, "Get up, take the child and his mother with
you and go back to the land of Israel, for those
21 who wanted to kill the child are dead." ·So
Joseph got up and, taking the child and his
mother with him, went back to the land of Israel.
22 But when he learned that Archelaus had succeeded
his father Herod as ruler of Judaea he was afraid
to go there, and being warned in a dream he left
23 for the region of Galilee. ·There he settled in a
town called Nazareth. In this way the words
spoken through the prophets were to be fulfilled:

> He will be called a Nazarene.

✠

Two startlingly different characters, Herod and Joseph, provide the framework for the story of how the
Messiah moves from Judea in the south to Galilee in
the north (13–23). Herod's rage drives the Messiah's
family into Egypt and keeps them there until his death.
Fear of Herod's equally vicious son Archelaus (who
would later be exiled to Gaul by the Romans because
of his cruelty) causes Joseph to bring his wife and son
to Galilee rather than Judea. Joseph's steadfast obedience is a counterpoint to Herod's hostility. The "just
one" is guided by dreams to protect the holy family
and eventually to set the stage for the major events of
the Gospel by bringing Jesus to Nazareth, in the northern district of Galilee, where most of Jesus' ministry
will take place.

Matthew's center of interest remains on Jesus. The

entire episode of Herod's frustrated rage and his slaughter of the infants recalls events surrounding the birth of Moses. Moses was the object of Pharaoh's vengeance and had to remain in hiding until the death of the Egyptian leader (Ex 2:15 to 4:31). Josephus, a Jewish historian contemporary with the writer of the Gospel, retells the story, including a slaughter of all male children and the detail that Moses' father received divine guidance in a dream. Moses gave the people God's Law on Sinai and led them from slavery to freedom. This portrayal of Moses as lawgiver and savior was the basic ingredient of his exceptional popularity in Jesus' own day. Matthew uses this image to shape his portrait of Jesus. A greater than Moses is here, one who will definitively reveal God's will and rescue his people from the shackles of death.

A series of Old Testament citations underwrite this Moses typology and carry the chapter to its finish. The fulfillment text of 2:15, a quotation from Hosea 11:1, punctuates the warning to Joseph and the subsequent flight into Egypt. The original passage in Hosea referred to the Exodus, the deliverance of the Jewish people from slavery. The quote is now applied by Matthew to Jesus ("my son") and not only refers to Jesus' eventual return from Egypt but subtly forecasts the definitive deliverance that a new Israel will experience through Jesus.

In verse 18, a fulfillment text of Jeremiah 31:15 provides a doleful commentary on Herod's slaughter of the Bethlehem children. This incident is not attested in any other records, but it does, in fact, accord with what is known of Herod's arbitrary and vicious character.

The Old Testament quote referred to the exile in the sixth century B.C. Ramah was a town north of Jerusalem and was on the supposed route the Jewish deportees took as they left their homeland. Matthew's use of this text may suggest several layers of meaning. It identifies Jesus with the great Jewish experience of exile (note how this event has already been singled out in the genealogy, cf. 1:11–12, 17) and introduces the foreboding prophecy of Jeremiah, a prophet whose prediction of woe against a faithless Israel will serve Matthew's purpose more than once in his Gospel (cf. 27:9–10). Finally, the original context of this citation is one of eventual rescue and comforting hope (cf. Jr 31:16ff.). Matthew may want to quietly remind his readers of Jesus' sure victory over pain and death.

The chapter closes with a somewhat puzzling citation that marks the arrival of Jesus and his family in Nazareth (23). The precise identity of the Old Testament text is difficult to pinpoint. It may be a free rendition of Isaiah 11:1, "a shoot springs from the stock of Jesse," which would involve a play on words between the Hebrew term for "shoot" (*nezir*) and the name of Jesus' home city. The Isaiah quotation was considered a prophecy defining the humble origins of the future Messiah, and this may have prompted Matthew's use of the text. Other commentators prefer a reference to Judges 13:5, "the boy shall be God's *nazirite* from his mother's womb." The text refers to Samson's vocation to be a *"nazir,"* a member of an association of strict asceticism and dedication in ancient Israel. Matthew might have exploited the play on words to single out Jesus' own devotion to his Messianic mission.

STUDY QUESTION: Matthew portrays Jesus as identified
with the deepest experiences of his
people: persecution, sorrow, exile,
Exodus. The Gospel invites us to
reflect on our own life experience
and to believe that the power of
Christ is present there, too.

JOHN: ELIJAH COME AGAIN

¹ 3 In due course John the Baptist appeared; he
preached in the wilderness of Judea and this
² was his message: ·"Repent, for the kingdom of
³ heaven is close at hand." ·This was the man the
prophet Isaiah spoke of when he said:

> A voice cries in the wilderness:
> prepare a way for the Lord,
> makes his path straight.

⁴ This man John wore a garment made of camel
hair with a leather belt around his waist, and
⁵ his food was locusts and wild honey. ·Then
Jerusalem and all Judaea and the whole Jordan
⁶ district made their way to him, ·and as they
were baptized by him in the river Jordan they
⁷ confessed their sins. ·But when he saw a number
of Pharisees and Sadducees coming for baptism
⁸ he said to them, ·"Brood of vipers, who warned
you to fly from the retribution that is coming?
But if you are repentant, produce the appropriate
⁹ fruit, ·and do not presume to tell yourselves, 'We
have Abraham for our father,' because, I tell you,
God can raise children for Abraham from these
¹⁰ stones. ·Even now the ax is laid to the roots of
the trees, so that any tree which fails to produce
good fruit will be cut down and thrown on the
¹¹ fire. ·I baptize you in water for repentance, but

the one who follows me is more powerful than
I am, and I am not fit to carry his sandals; he will
12 baptize you with the Holy Spirit and fire. ·His
winnowing fan is in his hand; he will clear his
threshing floor and gather his wheat into the
barn; but the chaff he will burn in a fire that will
never go out."

☩

So close and yet so different—this is John's role in
the entire Gospel tradition. Like Jesus, John senses
that a decisive moment is about to break over Israel
(cf. 3:2 and 4:17). Again like Jesus, John calls for
repentance and the proof of repentance in good deeds
(3:2, 9; 4:17; 7:16). Both John and Jesus will suffer
rejection, persecution, and even violent death (cf.
11:18–19).

But with equal insistence, the Gospels stress the absolute superiority of Jesus to John. John is a
forerunner, the promised Elijah who was expected to
precede the Messianic era (cf. Si 48:10–11); Jesus *is*
the Messiah. John announced the coming of the kingdom; Jesus inaugurated it. John's baptism was a ritual
of repentance; Jesus would baptize with the Spirit and
with fire, a gift that would forgive sins and quicken
new life. John prepared the way; Jesus *is* the way.

This blend of comparison and contrast helps the
reader prepare for the dramatic beginning of Jesus'
public ministry.

Matthew gives particular attention to the reception
John receives (5–6). Large crowds come to accept
John's baptism and thereby declare their intention to
reform their lives. The Pharisees and Sadducees are
singled out (7). These two Jewish groups, the Phari-

sees, lay reformers who stressed fidelity to the Law, and the Sadducees, a conservative aristocracy from whose ranks the Temple priests were chosen, become the chief opponents of Jesus in Matthew's Gospel. Although historically these two factions were often at loggerheads with each other, the evangelist lumps them together to typify the opposition of the Jewish leaders to the message of Jesus.

John scores them for the same type of failing that Jesus will accuse them of (cf. Ch. 23). They are hypocritical, claiming to be repentant but failing to show the genuineness of their conversion by a life of good deeds. They smugly point to their membership in God's chosen race but forget that fidelity, not race or class, is the only bond that binds one to God. The call to conversion involves responsibility. Those who respond will live a new life. Those who turn away or dissimulate will face judgment. The "axe is laid to the roots of the trees" (3:10).

Throughout the Gospel, the perfect image of what a disciple ought *not* to be will remain the Sadducees and, particularly, the Pharisees. One should keep in mind that Matthew's purpose was not to excoriate these Jewish leaders but to warn his *Christian* readers against adopting the attitudes these Gospel characters so notoriously exemplified.

STUDY QUESTION: Does the Gospel's indictment of the hypocrisy of the Sadducees and Pharisees have anything to say to me?

JESUS COMES TO THE JORDAN

¹³ Then Jesus appeared: he came from Galilee
¹⁴ to the Jordan to be baptized by John. ·John tried
to dissuade him. "It is I who need baptism from
¹⁵ you," he said, "and yet you come to me!" ·But
Jesus replied, "Leave it like this for the time
being; it is fitting that we should, in this way, do
all that righteousness demands." At this, John
gave in to him.
¹⁶ As soon as Jesus was baptized he came up
from the water, and suddenly the heavens opened
and he saw the Spirit of God descending like a
¹⁷ dove and coming down on him. ·And a voice
spoke from heaven, "This is my Son, the Beloved;
my favor rests on him."

⛨

"Then Jesus appeared." The moment has come. The
waiting is over. John had already stressed the pre-
eminence of Jesus in his words to the Sadducees and
Pharisees. Jesus is the "more powerful one," the one
who will baptize "with the Holy Spirit and fire" (cf.
11–12). Now, when Jesus takes his place, without pretense, in the crowds who shuffle forward to confess
their sins, John is compelled to protest his un-
worthiness (14).

For the first time in the Gospel Jesus speaks, and his words express a theme that Matthew will repeatedly emphasize: "we should . . . do all that righteousness demands" (15). There are two key words in the sentence: To "do all" (literally to "fulfill," the same Greek word Matthew so frequently uses regarding Jesus' fulfillment of Old Testament prophecies) and "righteousness," or justice. The latter term has a double layer of meaning in biblical thought. *God's* justice is his saving activity on behalf of his people. *Human* justice, or righteousness, is the effort we make to respond to God's goodness by carrying out his will.

It is possible that both levels of meaning are present in this keynote statement of Jesus. God's justice, or plan of salvation, is fulfilled by the very presence of John and Jesus in world history. At the same time, Jesus is a model of *human* righteousness as well, because he carries out God's plan of salvation by his loving fidelity to his Father's will. This emphasis on obedience to the will of God, on obedience perfectly modeled by Jesus, is a hallmark of Matthew's portrait of Christ.

The scene closes with the moment of baptism. Jesus' dedication to his mission is rewarded in a dramatic revelatory moment. The heavens open, God's own animating and powerful Spirit is seen to rest on Jesus, and the Father himself (with typical Jewish reverence, referred to only obliquely as "a voice from heaven") reveals to the crowds: "This is my Son. . . ." The words are a composite of Old Testament texts (cf. Ps 2:7; Is 42:1; Gn 22:2), and their message is clear: Jesus is the one who will bring God's own kingdom to realization. He will demonstrate what loyal obedience to God and genuine service to humankind are all about. He is *the* Son.

STUDY QUESTION: The keynote of Jesus' life is the fulfillment of all "righteousness." The Gospel challenges us: how do we characterize the fundamental motivation of our own lives?

Matthew 4:1–11
THE TESTING OF GOD'S SON

1,2 4 Then Jesus was led by the Spirit out into the wilderness to be tempted by the devil. ·He fasted for forty days and forty nights, after which
3 he was very hungry, ·and the tempter came and said to him, "If you are the Son of God, tell these
4 stones to turn into loaves." ·But he replied, "Scripture says:

> Man does not live on bread alone
> but on every word that comes from the mouth
> of God."

5 The devil then took him to the holy city and made him stand on the parapet of the Tem-
6 ple. ·"If you are the Son of God," he said, "throw yourself down; for Scripture says:

> He will put you in his angels' charge,
> and they will support you on their hands
> in case you hurt your foot against a stone."

7 Jesus said to him, "Scripture also says:

> You must not put the Lord your God to the
> test."

8 Next, taking him to a very high mountain, the devil showed him all the kingdoms of the world
9 and their splendor. ·"I will give you all these," he said, "if you fall at my feet and worship

10 me." ·Then Jesus replied, "Be off, Satan! For
Scripture says:

> You must worship the Lord your God,
> and serve him alone."

11 Then the devil left him, and angels appeared and
looked after him.

✠

The voice at the Jordan had publicly proclaimed
Jesus as God's Son. Now the quality of that sonship is
to be tested. The Spirit leads Jesus out into the "wilderness," that hauntingly beautiful and quietly danger-
ous expanse of desert that wraps itself around the
southern and eastern borders of Israel. The desert held
many memories for the Israelites. For Moses and their
forefathers, it had been a sandy bridge of rescue from
the slavery of Egypt to the possibilities of freedom in a
new land. But that ominous desert landscape also held
memories Israel might like to forget: constant murmur-
ing against Moses and the God he obeyed; a willing-
ness to abandon the march and return to Egypt; despair and infidelity which led to the idolatry of a calf of
gold.

Those collective memories must be recalled in order
to appreciate the point of this gospel passage. Both
Matthew and Luke present a version that greatly ex-
pands on a brief and cryptic scene in Mark (cf.
1:12–13). Their practically identical accounts (the
order of the second and third temptations are
switched) artfully exploit the Exodus memory. Jesus
fasts forty days, just as Moses did (Dt 9:9–18). All
of Jesus' replies to the temptation are taken verbatim
from Chapters 6 to 8 of The Book of Deuteronomy, a

key section, in which, at the end of the Exodus, Moses reminds his people of their covenant with Yahweh and the obedience this entails.

Each of the devil's attempts to subvert Jesus and his mission are turned away by a firm avowal of obedience. The sons and daughters of the ancient Exodus may have failed; *this* Son will not. He is asked to become a self-serving wonder-worker, flexing his power for his own ends (3). But Jesus' food is the bread of his Father's will (cf. Dt 8:3). He is taken to a pinnacle of the Temple and asked to probe the availability of God's provident care (cf. 6, where the devil quotes Ps 91). This temptation is shunted aside by a quotation of Dt 6:16, one should not "test" God since his care for his people is not in doubt. During the Exodus the Israelites had repeatedly challenged God's providence, as at Massah when they bluntly asked, "Is Yahweh with us, or not?" (cf. Ex 17:7).

These first two temptations were prefaced with the mocking clause "If you are the Son of God," a line that will have chilling echoes in the words of Jesus' mockers on Calvary (see 27:40). But the final temptation is the devil's naked plea for allegiance. Like a prospective buyer, Jesus is taken to a mountain and given a view of the kingdoms of this world. All of this might be his if he were to worship the right god. Jesus rejects the power of evil with the words of the first command of the Decalogue (Dt 6:13). There is only one power, only one God, and Jesus serves him alone. The Gospel will end with Jesus on another mountain (cf. 28:16ff.). All power on heaven and earth is given to him, not by the prince of evil, but by the Father. Jesus' authority will be derived not fron his control of this

world's kingdoms but from his absolute integrity and
his life-giving service.

The devil slinks away defeated, and angels, signs of
God's provident care, minister to Jesus (11). God's
Son has been tested and found worthy.

STUDY QUESTION: Jesus is faithful because he uses his
gifts to serve others, thereby ful-
filling God's will. To what or whom
have I dedicated the gifts of my life?
Am I a faithful son or daughter of
God?

Matthew 4:12–16
DAWN IN GALILEE

12 Hearing that John had been arrested he went
13 back to Galilee, ·and leaving Nazareth he went
and settled in Capernaum, a lakeside town on the
14 borders of Zebulun and Naphtali. ·In this way
the prophecy of Isaiah was to be fulfilled:

15 Land of Zebulun! Land of Naphtali!
Way of the sea on the far side of Jordan,
Galilee of the nations!
16 The people that lived in darkness
has seen a great light;
on those who dwell in the land and shadow of
death
a light has dawned.

☩

Jesus, the faithful Son, is now ready to begin his
life's work. This brief passage brings to a close the
"prologue" that Matthew has carefully assembled since
the beginning of Chapter 1. The verses are crammed
with geographical references and anchored with another "fulfillment" quotation (cf. above, p. 30), a combination reminiscent of the end of Chapter 2 (see
2:13–23). There, as here, we are told of Jesus on the
move. The threat of danger from Archelaus (see 2:22)

caused Jesus to come to Nazareth. Now, with a possible hint of danger in the arrest of John (12), Jesus comes to Capernaum, a small village on the northwestern shore of the Sea of Galilee, the base of operation for most of his ministry.

Matthew sees deep significance in this entry into Galilee. Here Jesus' words of wisdom and his acts of compassion would begin to heal a fractured world. Was it mere accident that it all began in Galilee, a district with an unusual proportion of gentiles and a part of Israel whose culture and orthodoxy were considered suspect by the Judeans to the south? No accident at all, in Matthew's view. Even the setting of Jesus' ministry foretells the shape of the kingdom: the "outsiders" will heed the Gospel. A carefully edited citation from Isaiah (8:23 to 9:1) makes the point: "Galilee of the nations," the gentiles, "on those who dwell in the land and shadow of death a light has dawned." Isaiah's original words said a light has "shone." But for Matthew this is only the beginning of the gospel, and the beginning of a new day is the dawn.

Matthew's Portrait of Jesus:
Wisdom Teacher, Compassionate Healer
Matthew 4:17 to 10:42

Matthew 4:17–25
THE KINGDOM OF HEAVEN IS CLOSE AT HAND

17 From that moment Jesus began his preaching with the message, "Repent, for the kingdom of heaven is close at hand."

18   As he was walking by the Sea of Galilee he saw two brothers, Simon, who was called Peter, and his brother Andrew; they were making a cast in the lake with their net, for they were 19 fishermen. ·And he said to them, "Follow me 20 and I will make you fishers of men." ·And they left their nets at once and followed him.

21   Going on from there he saw another pair of brothers, James son of Zebedee and his brother John; they were in their boat with their father Zebedee, mending their nets, and he called 22 them. ·At once, leaving the boat and their father, they followed him.

23   He went around the whole of Galilee teaching in their synagogues, proclaiming the Good News of the kingdom and curing all kinds of diseases 24 and sickness among the people. ·His fame spread throughout Syria, and those who were suffering from diseases and painful complaints of one kind or another, the possessed, epileptics, the paralyzed, were all brought to him, and he cured 25 them. ·Large crowds followed him coming from Galilee, the Decapolis, Jerusalem, Judaea and Transjordania.

✠

Matthew used the words of Isaiah to describe Jesus' ministry as "light" for those who live in darkness (16). The brilliance of that light will be displayed in a major section of the Gospel (Chs. 5–9), for which Matthew now prepares us.

The theme of this section is sounded in verse 17 and Matthew stresses its introduction by an emphatic time formula that is peculiar to his Gospel (cf. 16:21; 26:16). *"From that moment"* Jesus began his preaching: "Repent, for the kingdom of heaven is close at hand." The coming of the kingdom was a traditional way the Jews expressed their dream of an Israel that would be truly free, whole, and clothed in justice. Such a state of affairs could only be the work of God and of God's anointed one, the Messiah. The restorative work of bringing in the kingdom was the keynote of Jesus' own ministry. The things Jesus says and the acts he performs are understood as signs that at long last the promised age of the kingdom of God is about to break into the world.

Matthew will linger over Jesus' words and deeds in the five chapters that are to follow, and thereby build up a portrait of Jesus in a way unique among the four Gospels.

The preparatory verses of 4:18–25 help frame that portrait. Jesus' first act is to call disciples. Their summons is highly formalized, not unlike the "call narratives" of the Old Testament, in which prophet or king was swept into Yahweh's service. The crisp format indicates the meaning of "call." Discipleship is a gift of

God, and the proper response is willing obedience. Peter, who will play a prominent role in Matthew's Gospel, and Andrew, James, and John are called to share in Jesus' ministry, to be "fishers of men." Jesus' mission is not lingered over for its own sake. It is to be witnessed by the disciples, and as will be spelled out in Chapter 10, to be taken up by them and the community they represent.

Matthew's great portrait is previewed in verses 23-25, a sweeping summary of Jesus' ministry. Jesus' work is that of teaching and preaching the kingdom, of curing all kinds of diseases and sickness. Chapters 5 to 7, the famous Sermon on the Mount, will portray *Jesus the teacher*. Chapters 8 to 9, a collection of miracle stories, will portray *Jesus the healer*. The summary of the program cited in verse 23 will be repeated verbatim in 9:35, a clear indication of how deliberately Matthew constructs this crucial section of his Gospel.

Two final points should be noted about this summary passage. Matthew observes that Jesus teaches *"in their synagogues"* (23). Although the Gospel will eventually surge beyond the borders of Israel and be accepted by gentiles (cf. 28:19), it is first offered to Jews. They are the chosen people and Matthew has not lost his sense of continuity. Secondly, the target of Jesus' ministry is the vulnerable crowds who stream from all areas of Israel to hear him, "the possessed, epileptics, the paralyzed" (24). Jesus is not a detached dispenser of wisdom, nor a self-seeking wonder-worker, but what he says and what he does have one object: to make a suffering people whole.

Matthew 5:1–16
"JESUS BEGINS TO SPEAK"
THE BEATITUDES

[1] 5 Seeing the crowds, he went up the hill. There he sat down and was joined by his disci-
[2] ples. ·Then he began to speak. This is what he taught them:

[3]   "How happy are the poor in spirit;
       theirs is the kingdom of heaven.
[4]   Happy the gentle:
       they shall have the earth for their heritage.
[5]   Happy those who mourn:
       they shall be comforted.
[6]   Happy those who hunger and thirst for what is
          right:
       they shall be satisfied.
[7]   Happy the merciful:
       they shall have mercy shown them.
[8]   Happy the pure in heart:
       they shall see God.
[9]   Happy the peacemakers:
       they shall be called sons of God.
[10]   Happy those who are persecuted in the cause of
          right:
       theirs is the kingdom of heaven.

[11] "Happy are you when people abuse you and
   persecute you and speak all kinds of calumny

12 against you on my account. ·Rejoice and be glad,
    for your reward will be great in heaven; this is
    how they persecuted the prophets before you.
13 "You are the salt of the earth. But if salt be-
    comes tasteless, what can make it salty again? It
    is good for nothing, and can only be thrown out
    to be trampled underfoot by men.
14 "You are the light of the world. A city built
15 on a hilltop cannot be hidden. ·No one lights a
    lamp to put it under a tub; they put it on the
    lampstand where it shines for everyone in the
16 house. ·In the same way your light must shine
    in the sight of men, so that, seeing your good
    works, they may give the praise to your Father in
    heaven.

☩

Matthew sets this scene with care. Seeing the suffering and searching crowd, Jesus climbs a mountainside,
gathers his disciples about him, sits down, and begins
to speak. The deliberate ascent, the mountain setting,
and Jesus' position of authority (rabbis *sat* when
teaching), once again summon up Moses' image (cf.
Moses' ascent of Sinai to receive God's law for his people—Ex 19–20). A new Moses is here, and a new revelation of God's will is about to nourish that tattered
flock of humanity.

The "Sermon on the Mount," the loosely linked sayings that Matthew has collected in Chapters 5 to 7, begins with a series of Beatitudes," or blessings. They
form a "preamble" to Jesus' teaching, effectively dis-
tilling its essentials and pointing to the basic disposi-
tions needed to understand Jesus' message. This style
of speech was known from the Old Testament. Deuteronomy 27–28 strings together "Blessings" ("Happy

are . . .") and "woes" ("cursed are . . ."), which
describe the good or ill fortune that follows from keeping or breaking the Law. Ecclesiasticus (cf. 25:7–10)
and some of the prophets have similar lists. In Luke's
Gospel a more primitive listing of beatitudes is immediately followed by a series of woes (cf. Lk 6:20–26),
but in Matthew the woes are reserved for Chapter 23,
a section of the Gospel that functions almost as a negative counterpart to the Sermon on the Mount.

The first four Beatitudes might be considered together (3–6). The kinds of people declared "happy" in
this series recall the great prophecy of Isaiah 61:1ff.,
which foretells the Messiah's mission to the poor and
afflicted (the text is used in Lk 4:18 and seems to be
behind Mt 11:5). Each of these groups—the "poor in
spirit," the "gentle," or meek, the "mournful," those
who hunger and thirst for what is right—are promised
happiness or blessing *now* in view of a *future* reward.
The disciples of Jesus can begin to be happy now, because their future is so assured that its promised
gladness spills into the present. What keeps the Beatitudes from being empty mockeries of human suffering
is the authority of Jesus. Because Jesus is who he is,
his promises of blessing become themselves *cause* of
blessing. Thus at the very outset of the Sermon a fundamental theme of the Gospel has been sounded: Salvation is a gift, a gift whose creative power breaks into
our world of pain and darkness to make us whole and
blessed. Although Matthew will repeatedly insist on the
necessity of action in the Gospel, his even more fundamental insistence on salvation as a pure gift should not
be overlooked.

Matthew's rendition of the Beatitudes points to another side of the gospel. Those singled out for blessing

are not a particular social class, or mere inheritors of tragedy. Jesus' work with sinners and outcasts did not mean their poverty was a symptom of holiness. They were special objects of Jesus' mercy because they needed, and as God's people deserved, mercy. Their material and social deprivation also stood as vivid symbols of the absolute need and dependence that, in fact, describes the stance of all people before their God. But the poor and the outcasts could not presume on the gift of grace any more than the rich. To all, Jesus' message was two-edged. "The kingdom is at hand"—a promise of new life; but one must now live according to that gift, therefore "reform your lives."

Matthew brings out this attitudinal dimension of the Beatitudes more clearly than Luke's version does (cf. Lk 6:20–22). It is not simply the "poor," but the poor *in spirit,* not simply those "who hunger and thirst," but those "who hunger and thirst *for what is right."* These phrases are not meant to blunt the reality of Jesus' mission of justice to the poor. Instead, they amplify an essential dimension of God's kingdom: to be gifted by God demands a change of heart.

The next four Beatitudes (7–10)—all unique to Matthew—further illustrate the changed heart to which conversion leads. Each of the attitudes depicted becomes an important theme of Jesus' teaching in the Sermon and throughout the Gospel. Those who are merciful will receive mercy—a call for forgiveness and reconciliation that will be reflected in the Lord's Prayer (cf. 6:12, 14–15) and in Jesus' teaching on the relationship that must bind brethren together (cf. 5:23; 6:12, 14–15; 18:23–25). The "pure of heart," those whose actions are marked by absolute integrity, will see God—a call for sincerity Jesus will extend to one's

word (5:37), one's judgments (7:1–5), and to one's
piety (6:1–6, 16–18). The peacemakers, those who do
not perpetuate a cycle of violence (5:38–42), who refuse the sword (26:52–54), and who can accept the
most radical of Jesus' commands, "love your enemy"
(5:44–48), are promised the most breath-taking blessing of all: they shall be called "sons of God," because
such love fulfills God's ultimate command and creates
the deepest kinship with the Father (cf. 5:45–48).
Happy even those who suffer persecution "in the cause
of right" (or, literally, for the sake of righteousness or
justice), because, like the poor in spirit—like Jesus
himself—such giving and losing of life in the pursuit of
the Father's will is, mysteriously, to find life (16:25–
26).

The formation of true disciples is the purpose of
Jesus' teaching. The remaining Beatitudes (11–12)
and two striking metaphors that complete the Sermon's
preamble underline this. The address is no longer
"they" but "you," Jesus' audience of would-be followers. You are to rejoice in the sufferings you endure
for the sake of the gospel (11). You are to be salt and
light in a flat and dim world.

STUDY QUESTION: The Beatitudes put a question to
us: Can someone who is poor, gen-
tle, suffering, be truly "happy"?
Much of our world would say,
"No." Jesus teaches that the only
source of happiness worth yearning
for is a heart renewed by the gospel. Do we agree?

Matthew 5:17–20
JESUS AND THE LAW

17 "Do not imagine that I have come to abolish
the Law or the Prophets. I have come not to
18 abolish but to complete them. ·I tell you solemnly, till heaven and earth disappear, not one
dot, not one little stroke, shall disappear from
19 the Law until its purpose is achieved. ·Therefore,
the man who infringes even one of the least of
these commandments and teaches others to do
the same will be considered the least in the kingdom of heaven; but the man who keeps them
and teaches them will be considered great in the
kingdom of heaven.
20 "For I tell you, if your virtue goes no deeper
than that of the scribes and Pharisees, you will
never get into the kingdom of heaven.

✠

As we noted in the Introduction (see page 14),
Matthew writes his Gospel for a Jewish Christian community that found itself seemingly cut off from its heritage and adrift in a new and unexpected situation.
This passage, found only in Matthew's Gospel and
strategically placed at the very beginning of Jesus' own
authoritative teaching, attempts to place Jesus and the
Law in a context of continuity. Verse 17 lays out the

fundamental perspective: Jesus has come not to abolish or destroy the Law or the Prophets (the totality of the Jewish Scriptures in which God's will was revealed) but to "complete" them. "Complete" translates the Greek word for "fulfill," the identical verb used by Matthew to introduce the Old Testament fulfillment texts (cf. above, p. 30) and the word used in Jesus' opening statement in the Gospel (cf. 3:15). As the translation suggests, the word has the sense of completion, of accomplishing the purpose or goal God intended with the Law.

The time frame for this "completion" of the Law is expressed in verse 18. In fact, two separate time references are given: "till heaven and earth disappear" and "until its purpose is achieved."

When will this be? At the definite end of the world? In that case, the entire Jewish Law would still be in effect. But this does not seem possible, since in the course of the Gospel Jesus himself will nullify some points of the Law! The verse begins to make more sense when we grasp Matthew's sweeping view of history, a history that pivots around Jesus. The great drama of history in which God accomplishes the salvation of the world began with creation, quickened its pace in God's dealing with his chosen people and the gift of the Law, and will ring down its curtain with the end of the world. But the most decisive moment of world history is Jesus, and even more specifically, the great act of salvation accomplished through his death and resurrection. Jesus is the beginning of the end. All that God intended to say through creation, through Israel, and through the Law finds its ultimate expression in Jesus. All God's plans for the future have clearly been expressed in the person and mission of his Son.

Thus, for Matthew, the "passing away of heaven and earth" is, in a true sense, already here with Jesus. All things have been fulfilled; only Jesus and his teaching remain (cf. 24:35, where Matthew says precisely this). This is the reason for the vigorous demand of verse 20. The "virtue" of Jesus' disciples must go beyond that of the scribes and Pharisees, because the disciples are part of the new, and final, age of history. To come into contact with Jesus and his teaching is not only a privilege but a responsibility. This bracing command in view of a radically new consciousness also explains the call for integrity in verse 19. The text originally may have been used of the Jewish Law itself, but now the "law" understood here is *Jesus'* "law," which the Sermon and the rest of the Gospel will communicate. A favorite Matthaean theme is struck here: a call for sincerity that translates words into action. The one who *keeps and teaches* Jesus' commandments will be called greatest in the kingdom of heaven.

STUDY QUESTION: Matthew insists that Jesus' teaching fulfills all that God commands. What exactly is this new "law" of Jesus? What demand does Jesus Christ make on a person's life? This is the question the Gospel poses.

SYMPTOMS OF THE NEW HOLINESS

21 "You have learned how it was said to our
ancestors: You must not kill; and if anyone does
22 kill he must answer for it before the court. ·But
I say this to you: anyone who is angry with his
brother will answer for it before the court; if a
man calls his brother 'Fool' he will answer for it
before the Sanhedrin; and if a man calls him
23 'Renegade' he will answer for it in hell fire. ·So
then, if you are bringing your offering to the altar
and there remember that your brother has some-
24 thing against you, ·leave your offering there before the altar, go and be reconciled with your
brother first, and then come back and present
25 your offering. ·Come to terms with your oppo-
nent in good time while you are still on the way
to the court with him, or he may hand you over
to the judge and the judge to the officer, and you
26 will be thrown into prison. ·I tell you solemnly,
you will not get out till you have paid the last
penny.

27 "You have learned how it was said: You must
28 not commit adultery. ·But I say this to you: if
a man looks at a woman lustfully, he has already
29 committed adultery with her in his heart. ·If
your right eye should cause you to sin, tear it
out and throw it away; for it will do you less
harm to lose one part of you than to have your

30 whole body thrown into hell. ·And if your right
hand should cause you to sin, cut it off and throw
it away; for it will do you less harm to lose one
part of you than to have your whole body go to
hell.

31   "It has also been said: Anyone who divorces
32 his wife must give her a writ of dismissal. ·But I
say this to you: everyone who divorces his wife,
except for the case of fornication, makes her an
adulteress; and anyone who marries a divorced
woman commits adultery.

33   "Again, you have learned how it was said to
our ancestors: You must not break your oath,
34 but must fulfill your oaths to the Lord. ·But I
say this to you: do not swear at all, either by
35 heaven, since that is God's throne: ·or by the
earth, since that is his footstool; or by Jerusalem,
36 since that is the city of the great king. ·Do not
swear by your own head either, since you cannot
37 turn a single hair white or black. ·All you need
say is 'Yes' if you mean yes, 'No' if you mean
no; anything more than this comes from the evil
one.

38   "You have learned how it was said: Eye for
39 eye and tooth for tooth. ·But I say this to you:
offer the wicked man no resistance. On the contrary, if anyone hits you on the right cheek, offer
40 him the other as well; ·if a man takes you to law
and would have your tunic, let him have your
41 cloak as well. ·And if anyone orders you to go
42 one mile, go two miles with him. ·Give to anyone
who asks, and if anyone wants to borrow, do not
turn away.

43   "You have learned how it was said: You must
44 love your neighbor and hate your enemy. ·But I
say this to you: love your enemies and pray for
45 those who persecute you; ·in this way you will
be sons of your Father in heaven, for he causes
his sun to rise on bad men as well as good, and
his rain to fall on honest and dishonest men

46 alike. ·For if you love those who love you,
   what right have you to claim any credit? Even
47 the tax collectors do as much, do they not? ·And
   if you save your greetings for your brothers, are
   you doing anything exceptional? Even the pagans
48 do as much, do they not? ·You must therefore
   be perfect just as your heavenly Father is perfect."

☩

A deeper holiness is asked of the disciples of Jesus.
The expectation was spelled out in verse 20. Now it
will be forcefully illustrated by a series of six antithetical statements in which a command of the Law ("you
have learned how it was said to our ancestors . . .") is
contrasted with the escalated demands of the Gospel
("But *I* say this to you . . ."). A "new Moses" reveals
God's will to his people.

But it would be a mistake to conceive of Jesus as
substituting one law code (even a new and stricter
one) for another. The commands of Jesus as presented
by Matthew do not smack of legalism but are forceful
and concrete illustrations of the kind of integrity and
compassion instinctively striven for by one who senses
the meaning of the gospel. Each of the antitheses deals
with human relationships, and each makes clear that
being a follower of Jesus calls for a radically profound
understanding of one's relationship to other people.
Jesus came to restore a people to wholeness, and the
quality of his demands illustrates how complete that
restoration is to be.

The first antithesis (21–22) cites the command of
the Decalogue against murder (cf. Ex 20:13; Dt 5:17)
and refers to its legal sanction (cf. Ex 21:12). Jesus'

teaching reinforces the intent of the Law by scoring anger and alienation as the *roots* of violence. Therefore the disciple must make reconciliation an urgent priority, whether one is about to worship (23–24) or about to be embroiled in litigation (25–26).

The second antithesis also seeks to interiorize a command of the Law. It is not simply the overt act of infidelity that is destructive (cf. Ex 20:14; Dt 5:18) but the lustful heart (28). To look at a woman as an object of lust is to violate the respect due a human person. The jolting series of warnings that emphasize the seriousness of this demand (28–29) may have originally been used in another context (cf. Mk 9:43–48). Matthew may have appended these here because the radical and obviously hyperbolic call to eradicate any enticement to sin underlines the seriousness of mutual respect in Jesus' teaching.

In the third antithesis, the Jewish law (cf. Dt 24:1) governing procedure for divorce (and thus presuming its possibility) is directly countered by Jesus' own teaching (31–32). In the Gospels of Mark (10:11–12) and of Luke (16:18), Jesus' prohibition is without exception. The apparent qualification ("except for the case of fornication") introduced in Matthew's version is difficult to decipher. Jesus' teaching on divorce is repeated later in Matthew's Gospel, and the reader is referred to that text for a fuller discussion (cf. 19:3–12).

The Law called for the taking of an oath in conjunction with a religious vow or to testify to the truth of one's statement (e.g. Nb 30:3; Dt 23:22–24). A truly binding oath invoked God's name or a euphemism that obliquely referred to God (cf. the list Jesus cites in verses 34–36). The rabbis had cautioned against the

abuse of this practice, but Jesus' own command is still
more radical! "Do not swear at all" (34). The sincerity
and mutual respect that must characterize the disciples
of Jesus make a simple "yes" or a simple "no" a sacred
expression of truth.

The fifth antithesis cites the famous "law of talion"
(cf. Ex 21:24), "an eye for an eye and a tooth for a
tooth." The original intent of the law was to *limit* re-
venge by calling only for parity. But it was easily used
as a quasi-requirement for retribution, even when in
Jesus' own day that retribution would be primarily
financial rather than physical. Jesus' own command
once more "fulfils" a law by abrogating it, and insists
that aggression is to be absorbed, not returned. The illustration about going the "extra mile" in verse 41
probably refers to the highly resented capacity of the
Roman occupation forces to requisition a private citi-
zen to carry baggage or act as a guide. This antithesis
clearly distances Jesus from many of his contemporaries, who considered it a sacred duty to openly
resist the Romans. Here and in 26:52 violence is portrayed as alien to the Gospel.

This tone is amplified in the final and climactic antithesis of verses 43–48. The first portion of the old
Law quoted is from Lv 19:18, "you must love your
neighbor." The second half, "and hate your enemy," is
not found in the Hebrew Bible. However, it does
reflect the kind of particularistic thinking that defined
the concept of "neighbor" in first-century Judaism. The
members of the Jewish reform group at Qumran were
urged "to love the children of light" (i.e. members of
the community who observed the Law) and "to hate
the sons of darkness" (lawless Jews and gentiles). In a
society in which fidelity to the law was not only a

religious ideal but a source of national identity over
against a powerful and oppressive occupant, it is easy
enough to understand the stark terms in which the obligation to one's religion is put. This same social atmosphere reveals the incredible challenge of Jesus'
own command: "love your enemy." The "enemy" is
not remote (and therefore easy for one to be noble
about) but is as near and repugnant as the persecutor.

These verses bring us to the heart of Jesus' teaching
in the Gospel of Matthew. Almost all commentators
agree that the command "love your enemy" is the most
uniquely characteristic saying of Jesus. It has no parallel in biblical or other Jewish literature of the period.
The statements that follow this command (45–48)
amplify and confirm the centrality of this antithesis. To
love an enemy is to demonstrate that one is a "son of
your Father in heaven." God's love is indiscriminate
and gratuitous; his sun rises on good and bad, his rain
falls on honest and dishonest. The traditional theme of
imitation of God, used in biblical (cf. Lv 19:2) and
pagan literature as well, is employed here to illustrate
the importance of the love command. A person is most
like the Father when he or she does not pen love
within the comfortable boundaries of reciprocity (46).
The "tax collector" and the "pagan," indicative of the
"unconverted" person, can do as much. But the disciple is called to do more: to love even his enemy, and
thus to be "perfect" as the heavenly Father is perfect.
The word "perfect" translates the Greek word *teleios,*
which has the connotation of "wholeness" or "com-
pleteness." The disciple experiences "wholeness" when
he or she is animated by the kind of love that allows
one to love even an enemy. Later in the Gospel, the
same word, perfect, will be defined as "following Jesus"

(cf. 19:21). That is really an alternate way of express-
ing the love-of-enemy command, because in the Gospel
Jesus is portrayed as carrying out his own teaching
with absolute integrity.

STUDY QUESTION: The core of Jesus' teaching is his
command: "love your enemy."
Does this summarize our own understanding of what Christianity really means?

Matthew 6:1–18
ON DOING GOOD FOR
YOUR FATHER TO SEE

1 6 "Be careful not to parade your good deeds before men to attract their notice; by doing this you will lose all reward from your Father in
2 heaven. ·So when you give alms, do not have it trumpeted before you; this is what the hypocrites do in the synagogues and in the streets to win men's admiration. I tell you solemnly, they have
3 had their reward. ·But when you give alms, your left hand must not know what your right is
4 doing; ·your almsgiving must be secret, and your Father who sees all that is done in secret will reward you.

5 "And when you pray, do not imitate the hypocrites: they love to say their prayers standing up in the synagogues and at the street corners for people to see them. I tell you solemnly, they have
6 had their reward. ·But when you pray, go to your private room and, when you have shut your door, pray to your Father who is in that secret place, and your Father who sees all that is done in secret will reward you.

7 "In your prayers do not babble as the pagans do, for they think that by using many words they
8 will make themselves heard. ·Do not be like them; your Father knows what you need before
9 you ask him. ·So you should pray like this:

"Our Father in heaven,
may your name be held holy,
10   your kingdom come,
your will be done,
on earth as in heaven.
11   Give us today our daily bread.
12   And forgive us our debts,
as we have forgiven those who are in debt to us.
13   And do not put us to the test,
but save us from the evil one.

14 Yes, if you forgive others their failings, your
15 heavenly Father will forgive you yours; ·but if
you do not forgive others, your Father will not
forgive your failings either.
16   "When you fast do not put on a gloomy look
as the hypocrites do: they pull long faces to let
men know they are fasting. I tell you solemnly,
17 they have had their reward. ·But when you fast,
18 put oil on your head and wash your face, so that
no one will know you are fasting except your Father who sees all that is done in secret; and your
Father who sees all that is done in secret will
reward you.

Fulfilling God's commands is also the concern of this
section of the Sermon. The opening verse spells out
this theme: our "good deeds" must not be an empty
show but must proceed from an absolutely sincere
heart. Matthew categorizes "good deeds" according to
the three traditional works of Judaism: almsgiving,
prayer, and fasting. A rigorous contrasting pattern
(not unlike the antithetical form of 5:21–48) decries
the "good deeds" of the "hypocrites," which are done
in public to attract attention, and then proposes Jesus'
own teaching (note the authoritative *"I tell you*

solemnly . . ." in verses 2, 5, 16), which insists that
good works must be wholly dedicated to the Father.

Almsgiving (1–4) was a highly developed and admi-
rable part of Jewish tradition. Jesus did not abrogate it
but insists that it not be accompanied by the trumpets
of hypocrisy. Alms should be given "in secret," that is
as an expression of true love whose reward is assured
by the Father. A patterned life of deep prayer was also
a treasure of the Jewish heritage. Jesus' words, effectively contrasting the public arena of synagogue and
street corner with the unpretentious privacy of a room
in a house, call for a piety that does not keep one eye
on the applause meter but is a sincere and serious com-
munication with the Father (5–6). Fasting, another
traditional Jewish practice adopted by the Christians, is
not to be an empty asceticism that attempts to cower
others through subtle pride. Genuine fasting should
free one to be of service (16–18), and to be even festive in the process.

Praying does not mean "babbling" (7), the piling up
of phrases and formulas to ensure a hearing, as much
of the pagan and even some of the Jewish prayers of
this period did. To do so is to subtly hope that one's
language might control God. The same sincerity and
straightforwardness that should rule almsgiving and
fasting must guide the tone of one's prayer.

The Lord's Prayer (9–13) is offered as a pattern of
sincere prayer. Some of its petitions are similar in content to a Jewish prayer, the *Shemoneh Esreh,* recited
twice daily in the synagogue. But the bold directness of
the Our Father bears the authoritative stamp of its ultimate author, Jesus.

The disciples are directed to address God as "Father," sharing in Jesus' own intimate filial relationship

(cf. 11:25–30). Matthew's own community may have added the phrase "in heaven" (it is missing in Luke's version) to stress the sense of awe and reverence that must paradoxically coexist with the Christian's unprecedented access to God. The first three petitions (9–10) state in alternate ways the same basic hope: a prayer that the Father's power would establish in the world of humankind the same network of peace, unity, and love that exists in God's own kingdom.

The same directness and instinct for the essential characterizes the remaining three petitions (11–13), which shift from a future and outer-directed "your name," "your kingdom," "your will," to the palpable needs of the believer: "our bread," "our debts," "save us." Jesus' prayer is not utopian. The plea for "daily bread" is probably best understood as just that: a prayer for basic human sustenance. Because the unusual Greek word for "daily" can also mean "future" or literally "tomorrow's" bread, some believe that the bread referred to is symbolic of the kingdom and not just physical food. But the practical tones of the prayer and Jesus' own concern for feeding (cf. 14:13–21; 15:32–38) and healing (Chs. 8–9) make the more prosaic interpretation the preferred one.

Another consuming concern of Jesus' ministry is expressed in a petition calling for forgiveness. This is the only petition that includes a *condition:* "as we have forgiven those who are in debt to us" (12). The absolute centrality of reconciliation in Jesus' teaching and his insistence that genuine communion with the Father brings a new understanding of our relationship with each other is reinforced by the repetition of this theme at the end of the prayer (14–15) and at other key points in the Gospel (cf. 7:12; 18:21–25).

The prayer ends with a petition that we not be put to the "test" and that we be delivered from the "evil one" (13). Suffering and death can overwhelm us, and therefore we ask the one in whose hands the ultimate destiny of the world rests not to "tempt us" beyond our strength. The tone of this petition (and the entire prayer) is not unlike the temptation scene of 4:1–11, where Jesus turned aside the enticements of evil by affirming his total dedication to his Father. The prayer will be evoked again as Jesus faces his final test in Gethsemane (see 26:42).

STUDY QUESTION: As Christians, we pray and give alms and even fast. The Gospel endorses these practices only if they derive from a free and festive communion with our Father. How does our piety stand up?

Matthew 6:19–34
THE PERILS OF A DIVIDED HEART

¹⁹ "Do not store up treasures for yourselves on earth, where moths and woodworms destroy them ²⁰ and thieves can break in and steal. ·But store up treasures for yourselves in heaven, where neither moth nor woodworms destroy them and ²¹ thieves cannot break in and steal. ·For where your treasure is, there will your heart be also.

²² "The lamp of the body is the eye. It follows that if your eye is sound, your whole body will ²³ be filled with light. ·But if your eye is diseased, your whole body will be all darkness. If then, the light inside you is darkness, what darkness that will be!

²⁴ "No one can be the slave of two masters: he will either hate the first and love the second, or treat the first with respect and the second with scorn. You cannot be the slave both of God and of money.

²⁵ "That is why I am telling you not to worry about your life and what you are to eat, nor about your body and how you are to clothe it. Surely life means more than food, and the body ²⁶ more than clothing! ·Look at the birds in the sky. They do not sow or reap or gather into barns; yet your heavenly Father feeds them. Are you ²⁷ not worth much more than they are? ·Can any of you, for all his worrying, add one single cubit to ²⁸ his span of life? ·And why worry about clothing?

Think of the flowers growing in the fields; they
29 never have to work or spin; ·yet I assure you that
not even Solomon in all his regalia was robed like
30 one of these. ·Now if that is how God clothes the
grass in the field which is there today and thrown
into the furnace tomorrow, will he not much
more look after you, you men of little faith?
31 So do not worry; do not say, 'What are we to
eat? What are we to drink? How are we to be
32 clothed?' ·It is the pagans who set their hearts
on all these things. Your heavenly Father knows
33 you need them all. ·Set your hearts on his kingdom first, and on his righteousness, and all these
34 other things will be given you as well. ·So do not
worry about tomorrow: tomorrow will take care
of itself. Each day has enough trouble of its own.

✠

This portion of the Sermon makes a connection between two important concerns: singlehearted dedication to the kingdom, and the practical needs of every-
day living. The Gospel does not ignore the practical
necessities of food and clothing but places these cares
in the perspective of faith.

The evangelist brings together a series of originally
independent sayings and metaphors. The first (19–21)
picks up the theme of "heavenly reward" from the previous section (cf. 6:1–18) and calls for a faith-wise
use of possessions. Anxious padding of one's own
wealth is ultimately quite vulnerable to destruction
(19–20). Use of one's energy and resources for the
kingdom is the only security worth striving for.

The theme of dedicating one's life to the kingdom is
restated (22–23) in the metaphor of a "sound eye" as
a clear lens through which God's light can flood the
whole body. Like tasteless salt (another of Jesus'

arresting metaphors), inner light that turns out to be
darkness vividly portrays the futility of a life dedicated
to an unworthy goal.

The third metaphor (24) is more explicit. No one
can attempt to put priority on God *and* possessions
without suffering from a divided heart.

The section concludes with one of the sermon's most
lyrical passages (25–34). Since our bodies and the life
that animates them are gifts from God, we should not
be concerned with the cares of food and clothing as if
God did not exist. Nature's own beauty challenges the
mentality that devotes anxious and all-consuming attention to one's own material security. Such an attitude
springs from "little faith," a quaint and effective characterization of imperfect discipleship that Matthew will
utilize repeatedly in his Gospel (cf. 8:26; 14:31; 16:8;
17:20). The follower of Jesus is to husband his or her
energies and care for doing God's will (33). Thus this
passage is not an invitation to passivity, nor does it
spring from a trivial romanticism about nature and its
beauty. These verses, and the entire section they conclude, are a call for action—action that proceeds from
commitment to the kingdom. Such commitment frees
one to live fully in the present and not to be im-
mobilized or diverted by anxiety about one's future
(34).

STUDY QUESTION: The Gospel again challenges us
about the fundamental priorities of
our lives. Are we "anxious" about
the right things? Do we dedicate
our lives to things that are worthy
of us?

Matthew 7:1–12
THE BOND OF MERCY

1 7 "Do not judge, and you will not be judged;
2 because the judgments you give are the judgments you will get, and the amount you measure
3 out is the amount you will be given. ·Why do
you observe the splinter in your brother's eye and
4 never notice the plank in your own? ·How dare
you say to your brother, 'Let me take the splinter
out of your eye,' when all the time there is a
5 plank in your own? ·Hypocrite! Take the plank
out of your own eye first, and then you will see
clearly enough to take the splinter out of your
brother's eye.

6   "Do not give dogs what is holy; and do not
throw your pearls in front of pigs, or they may
trample them and then turn on you and tear you
to pieces.

7   "Ask, and it will be given to you; search, and
you will find; knock, and the door will be opened
8 to you. ·For the one who asks always receives;
the one who searches always finds; the one who
knocks will always have the door opened to him.
9 Is there a man among you who would hand his
10 son a stone when he asked for bread? ·Or would
11 hand him a snake when he asked for a fish? ·If
you, then, who are evil, know how to give your
children what is good, how much more will your
Father in heaven give good things to those who
ask him!

12   "So always treat others as you would like them
      to treat you; that is the meaning of the Law and
      the Prophets.

⚓

The central section of the Sermon (6:1 to 7:12)
now begins to slant to its conclusion. An exhortation
not to "judge" a brother (7:1–5) reminds the hearers
of the principle of reciprocity: As we judge, so we will
be judged. Awareness of our relationship to God
should bring new understanding of our relationship to
each other, a relationship that must be ruled by understanding and compassion, not the cold arrogance of
judgment.

Verse 5 begins to move beyond the single emphasis
of the prohibition against judging (1). There is a
difference between the hypocritical judgment of another and the genuine concern to correct or admonish
an erring brother or sister. But self-deception can easily make "fraternal correction" a deft proclamation of
one's own superiority. Only one whose eye is plank-
free, who has admitted the need for repentance and
conversion, is able to correct someone else with respect
and compassion (5).

The saying in verse 6 may have originally been used
in the context of Jewish-gentile tensions. "Dogs" and
"pigs" were both used as disparaging terms for gentiles.
And this saying may have been contrived as a caution
against sharing sacred laws and institutions with those
who would not understand or respect them. But in the
context of the Sermon, it seems to pick up the final ad-
monition of verse 5. The call for compassion and understanding does not eliminate the need for discrim-

ination and reverence. The *Didache,* a Christian
writing which may be almost contemporary with
Matthew's Gospel, uses a similar saying to warn
against sharing bread blessed at the agape meals with
the "unholy."

The call for persevering prayer (7–11) seems at first
glance to be dislocated from Matthew's earlier consideration of prayer (6:5–15). But, in fact, it blends into
the conclusion of this section of the Sermon. The
demand for absolute sincerity in our good deeds
(6:1–18), for the single-minded dedication of our
energies and our resources to God's will (6:19–34),
and for compassionate (7:1–5) and prudent (7:6)
dealings with our brethren revives one's sense of impotence before the exacting demands of the gospel. Fidelity is a gift that should be sought with the same
sense of need and trust as a child asks his father for
bread (9–10). Although Matthew continues to insist
on action and good deeds as the touchstone of genuine
fidelity, he is equally insistent that the ability to respond to the gospel is a gift.

The expository part of the Sermon concludes with
the key saying of verse 12, the so-called "golden rule."
This emphasis on the "love command" and its interpretation as the "meaning of the Law and the Prophets" parallels the conclusion of the first major section
of the Sermon (cf. 5:43–48). The climax of Jesus'
own interpretation of the Law is the command to "love
your enemy." Loving one's enemy, treating others as
you would like them to treat you—this is how Jesus'
own teaching fulfills the purpose of the Law (cf.
5:17). Matthew will repeat this crucial stance of the
Gospel in 22:34–40.

STUDY QUESTION: Once again, the teaching of Jesus slips into a single, clear focus: "treat others as you would like them to treat you." Does my Christian life make a difference in the way I treat others?

A CALL FOR FIDELITY

13 "Enter by the narrow gate, since the road that leads to perdition is wide and spacious, and many 14 take it; ·but it is a narrow gate and a hard road that leads to life, and only a few find it.

15 "Beware of false prophets who come to you disguised as sheep but underneath are ravenous 16 wolves. ·You will be able to tell them by their fruits. Can people pick grapes from thorns, or figs 17 from thistles? ·In the same way, a sound tree pro- 18 duces good fruit but a rotten tree bad fruit. ·A sound tree cannot bear bad fruit, nor a rotten 19 tree bear good fruit. ·Any tree that does not pro- duce good fruit is cut down and thrown on the 20 fire. ·I repeat, you will be able to tell them by their fruits.

21 "It is not those who say to me, 'Lord, Lord,' who will enter the kingdom of heaven, but the per- son who does the will of my Father in heaven. 22 When the day comes many will say to me, 'Lord, Lord, did we not prophesy in your name, cast out demons in your name, work many miracles 23 in your name?' ·Then I shall tell them to their faces: I have never known you; away from me, you evil men!"

24 "Therefore, everyone who listens to these words of mine and acts on them will be like a sensible 25 man who built his house on rock. ·Rain came

down, floods rose, gales blew and hurled themselves against that house, and it did not fall: it
26 was founded on rock. ·But everyone who listens
to these words of mine and does not act on them
will be like a stupid man who built his house on
27 sand. ·Rain came down, floods rose, gales blew
and struck that house, and it fell; and what a fall
it had!"
28   Jesus had now finished what he wanted to say,
and his teaching made a deep impression on the
29 people ·because he taught them with authority,
and not like their own scribes.

⊹

The Sermon on the Mount concludes with a string of
paired images. There are two "ways" (13–14), two
kinds of trees and two kinds of fruit (15–20), two
kinds of responses (21–23), two kinds of house builders (24–27). Each pair illustrates the need for decisive
response to the teaching of Jesus and the consequences
of such response. This theme, of action and responsibility, is a major motif of Matthew's Gospel.

The string begins with the image of the two ways
(13–14), a traditional metaphor in the Bible for one's
life choice (cf. Dt 30:15–20). The narrowness of the
road to life and the reference to the "few" who find it
illustrate once again how fidelity is ultimately a gift of
God. The test of good deeds is used to unmask "false
prophets" (15–20). Early Christianity brimmed with
vitality and benefited from many prophetic types in its
midst. These inspired preachers and healers apparently
adopted Jesus' own itinerant life-style, preaching the
gospel from town to town. But such a free-lance corps
of missionaries also produced abuses, people whose
miraculous powers were impressive credentials but

whose brand of Christianity was, in fact, divisive and misleading. Matthew's community applied the same test of genuineness to the charismatic prophets that it did to all disciples: "You will be able to tell them by their fruits" (7:16, 20).

The following paragraph (21–23) probably refers to the same situation. Matthew's criterion is consistent. It is not enough to cry out in prayer, "Lord, Lord," nor even to prophesy or to work cures in Jesus' name. The ultimate test is the one that Jesus himself perfectly exemplifies: to do "the will of my Father in heaven" (21). Those who are false disciples must bear the consequences. These "evil men" (literally "doers of lawlessness") will have no kinship with Jesus. This way (23) of speaking about judgment is quite similar to the Matthaean judgment scene of the sheep and the goats (cf. below 25:31ff.).

The concluding metaphor—the two ways of building a house (24–27)—illustrates Matthew's definition of a disciple: one who "listens to these words of mine and acts on them" (24). The life constructed by such a truly sensible person will withstand the rigors of judgment.

The Sermon is terminated with a formula ("Jesus had now finished what he wanted to say . . ." [28]) that appears five times in the Gospel, each example concluding a major discourse of Jesus and orientating the reader back to the flow of the narrative (cf. 11:1, after the mission discourse; 13:53, after the parable discourse; 19:1, after the discourse on community; and 26:1, at the end of Jesus' last discourse). In this case, the transitional formula is fortified by a reference to Jesus' impression on the crowd (28–29). Jesus' "authority" derives not only from the impact of his penetrating wisdom but from his identity. He is not a scribe of the old order but the Son whose teaching reveals the Father's will and whose own life is the perfect example of the fidelity he demands.

STUDY QUESTION: Matthew writes a Gospel for "doers," for those who do not simply say the right words or perform the proper gestures but who really carry out the commands of Jesus into the practical decisions of their lives. The Church still needs to listen soberly to the indictment of those who cry, "Lord, Lord," but do not do the will of the Father.

Matthew 8:1–17
"I WANT TO [CURE]"
THE POWER OF JESUS

1 8 After he had come down from the mountain
2 8 large crowds followed him. ·A leper now came
up and bowed low in front of him. "Sir," he
3 said, "if you want to, you can cure me." ·Jesus
stretched out his hand, touched him and said, "Of
course I want to! Be cured!" And his leprosy was
4 cured at once. ·Then Jesus said to him, "Mind
you do not tell anyone, but go and show yourself to the priest and make the offering prescribed
by Moses, as evidence for them."

5 When he went into Capernaum a centurion
6 came up and pleaded with him. ·"Sir," he said,
"my servant is lying at home paralyzed, and in
7 great pain." ·"I will come myself and cure him,"
8 said Jesus. ·The centurion replied, "Sir, I am not
worthy to have you under my roof; just give the
9 word and my servant will be cured. ·For I am
under authority myself, and have soldiers under
me; and I say to one man: Go, and he goes; to
another: Come here, and he comes; to my ser-
10 vant: Do this, and he does it." ·When Jesus heard
this he was astonished and said to those following
him, "I tell you solemnly, nowhere in Israel have
11 I found faith like this. ·And I tell you that many
will come from east and west to take their places
with Abraham and Isaac and Jacob at the feast in

¹² the kingdom of heaven; ·but the subjects of the kingdom will be turned out into the dark, where
¹³ there will be weeping and grinding of teeth." ·And to the centurion Jesus said, "Go back, then; you have believed, so let this be done for you." And the servant was cured at that moment.
¹⁴ And going into Peter's house Jesus found Pe-
¹⁵ ter's mother-in-law in bed with fever. ·He touched her hand and the fever left her, and she got up and began to wait on him.
¹⁶ That evening they brought him many who were possessed by devils. He cast out the spirits with a
¹⁷ word and cured all who were sick. ·This was to fulfill the prophecy of Isaiah:

> He took our sicknesses away and carried our diseases for us.

✠

At the beginning of the Sermon on the Mount, Matthew stressed that the crowds who swarmed around Jesus were wracked with suffering and disease (see 4:24–25). These same crowds who thrilled to Jesus' teaching (7:28–29) will now witness the power of his compassion. Matthew completes his portrait of Jesus by using the next two chapters (8:1 to 9:37) to depict him as one who not only teaches with authority but heals with love.

Three crisp miracle stories form the first unit of this section. The unit's conclusion, a brief summary of Jesus' activity and a quotation (16–17) from Isaiah 53:4, trumpets the theme: Jesus is God's Servant, whose power to heal lifts the burden of sickness and sin from a suffering people. This is the savior Jesus announced in the infancy Gospel (see 1:21). This is the obedient Son who refused to use his power for self-aggrandizement in the desert test (see 4:3–6).

The trim lines of the stories of the leper's cure (8:1–4) and of the healing of Peter's mother-in-law (8:14–15) effectively stress Jesus' power. The leper reverences Jesus (literally "genuflects" before him) and addresses him as "sir," using the Greek word *kyrie,* a Christian title affirming the divine power of Jesus (cf. 8:2). The dialogue is terse, climaxing in Jesus' majestic "I want to! Be cured." In the third miracle, Jesus strides into the house and cures Peter's mother-in-law with a touch.

The cure of the centurion's servant (8:5–13), the only story of these two chapters not found in Mark, also emphasizes the power of Jesus. The centurion's deference to Jesus and their conversation about authority effectively make this point. The fact that the man is a gentile also helps Matthew bring to the surface a strong undercurrent of the Gospel. The response of this gentile to Jesus is a sign of the future, when outsiders from the east and the west will share in the Messianic banquet, while those who presume their right to be there will be turned away (10–13).

But Jesus has not rejected his people. Even as he performs his acts of power, he abides by the Law in reminding the leper to verify his cure with the Temple priests and to make the prescribed offering demanded by the Law (cf. Lv 14:2ff.).

STUDY QUESTION: Jesus has the power to heal. Is this a magic power unleashed only in the village of Capernaum, or does the risen Christ still have the power to heal me?

IN THE WAKE OF A HOMELESS JESUS

18 When Jesus saw the great crowds all about him
19 he gave orders to leave for the other side. ·One
of the scribes then came up and said to him,
"Master, I will follow you wherever you go."
20 Jesus replied, "Foxes have holes and the birds of
the air have nests, but the Son of Man has nowhere to lay his head."

21 Another man, one of his disciples, said to him,
22 "Sir, let me go and bury my father first." ·But
Jesus replied, "Follow me, and leave the dead to
bury their dead."

23 Then he got into the boat followed by his dis-
24 ciples. ·Without warning a storm broke over the
lake, so violent that the waves were breaking right
25 over the boat. But he was asleep. ·So they went to
him and woke him saying, "Save us, Lord, we
26 are going down!" ·And he said to them, "Why
are you so frightened, you men of little faith?"
And with that he stood up and rebuked the winds
27 and the sea; and all was calm again. ·The men
were astounded and said, "Whatever kind of man
is this? Even the winds and the sea obey him."

28 When he reached the country of the Gadarenes
on the other side, two demoniacs came toward
him out of the tombs—creatures so fierce that
29 no one could pass that way. ·They stood there
shouting, "What do you want with us, Son of
God? Have you come here to torture us before

30 the time?" ·Now some distance away there was a
31 large herd of pigs feeding, ·and the devils pleaded
with Jesus, "If you cast us out, send us into the
32 herd of pigs." ·And he said to them, "Go then,"
and they came out and made for the pigs; and at
that the whole herd charged down the cliff into
33 the lake and perished in the water. ·The swine-
herds ran off and made for the town, where they
told the whole story, including what had hap-
34 pened to the demoniacs. ·At this the whole town
set out to meet Jesus; and as soon as they saw
him they implored him to leave the neighborhood.

1 9 He got back in the boat, crossed the water and
2   came to his own town. ·Then some people appeared, bringing him a paralytic stretched out on
a bed. Seeing their faith, Jesus said to the paralytic, "Courage, my child, your sins are forgiven."
3 And at this some scribes said to themselves, "This
4 man is blaspheming." ·Knowing what was in their
minds Jesus said, "Why do you have such wicked
5 thoughts in your hearts? ·Now, which of these is
easier: to say, 'Your sins are forgiven,' or to say,
6 'Get up and walk?' ·But to prove to you that the
Son of Man has authority on earth to forgive
sins,"—he said to the paralytic—"get up, and
7 pick up your bed and go off home." ·And the man
8 got up and went home. ·A feeling of awe came
over the crowd when they saw this, and they
praised God for giving such power to men.

9   As Jesus was walking on from there he saw
a man named Matthew sitting by the customs
house, and he said to him, "Follow me." And he
got up and followed him.

10   While he was at dinner in the house it happened that a number of tax collectors and sinners
came to sit at the table with Jesus and his disci-
11 ples. ·When the Pharisees saw this, they said to
his disciples, "Why does your master eat with

¹² tax collectors and sinners?" ·When he heard this
he replied, "It is not the healthy who need the
¹³ doctor, but the sick. ·Go and learn the meaning
of the words: What I want is mercy, not sacrifice.
And indeed I did not come to call the virtuous,
but sinners."

¹⁴   Then John's disciples came to him and said,
"Why is it that we and the Pharisees fast, but
¹⁵ your disciples do not?" ·Jesus replied, "Surely
the bridegroom's attendants would never think of
mourning as long as the bridegroom is still with
them? But the time will come for the bridegroom
to be taken away from them, and then they will
¹⁶ fast. ·No one puts a piece of unshrunken cloth
onto an old cloak, because the patch pulls away
¹⁷ from the cloak and the tear gets worse. ·Nor do
people put new wine into old wineskins; if they
do, the skins burst, the wine runs out, and the
skins are lost. No; they put new wine into fresh
skins and both are preserved."

✠

As Jesus is about to get into the boat (18–22), a
scribe and a disciple provide the occasion for Jesus'
warning about the rigors of discipleship, another major
theme of the miracle section. The scribe's bold and apparently unconsidered declaration ("I will follow you
wherever you go") is brought up short by Jesus' reminder of the homelessness of the "Son of Man" (a
title particularly associated in the Gospels with Jesus'
death). The cost of the Christian mission will be
spelled out further in 10:6–25. A disciple who begs
leave to bury his father, an obvious sacred duty in Judaism, is met with Jesus' own unflinching demand that
the gospel, i.e. following Jesus, be put first above all

things. Jesus is *the* way of life; anything less is "to join ranks with the dead."

The story of the calming of the storm (23–27), the first of three miracles in this section, continues the boat motif. Matthew's rendition of this story will make a touching image of the church. The disciples "follow" (almost a technical term for discipleship) Jesus into the boat and, once at sea, begin to experience a violent storm (24, literally a giant "earthquake," a term often used to describe the troubles the community will encounter in the final age). Fear of the raging sea moves them to pray, "Save us, Lord" (again a title referring to Jesus' divine power). This is quite different from Mark's version, in which the disciples rebuke Jesus for being asleep (cf. Mk 4:38)! Jesus responds by asserting his majestic power over the chaos of the sea (the same power attributed to Yahweh in the Old Testament, cf. Ps 29:3; 65:8; 89:9; 93:4; 107:29) and by gently characterizing that frightened boat crew as "men of little faith" (cf. above, 6:30).

Two other miracles complete the trilogy. Matthew has radically shortened the colorful story of the Gadarene demoniacs (compare Mk 5:1–20), focusing on the demons' terrified recognition of what they face (29). Jesus is "Son of God" and his ministry of healing and teaching anticipates the final destruction of evil.

The cure of the paralytic (9:1–8) has also been clipped by Matthew, and again the purpose is a sharper focus on Jesus' authority. This story may have originally combined a healing story with a controversy about Jesus' power to forgive sins. The latter has become the central point in Matthew's version (9:6). As in the stilling of the storm, so here the evangelist keeps

one eye on the community's own experience as well as
on the history of Jesus. The reaction of the crowd (8),
praising God "for giving such power to *men*," suggests
that the controversy between Jesus and the scribes over
the power to forgive sins now mirrors later tension between Matthew's church, which claimed such power,
and the objection of the synagogue.

The theme of discipleship, which began this section,
is strongly reasserted at its conclusion. The implicit rejection of Jesus in the protests of the scribes is countered by the instant discipleship of Matthew the tax
collector (9:9); and Jesus' table fellowship with sinners (10) is opposed by the Pharisees. Jesus' citation
of Hosea 6:6 in verse 13 (to be repeated in 12:7)
stifles their murmurs against his ministry by reasserting
the primacy of compassion over the less important stip-
ulations of the Law (the connotation of "sacrifice," in
this context). Matthew presents Jesus as carrying out
with rigorous integrity his own teaching (7:12).

A final objection concludes this segment. John's disciples challenge the followers of Jesus on their failure
to fast (14–17). The link with the previous material is
the authority of Jesus and his ministry. Just as his
teaching on love and his works of compassion radically
fulfill the Law and cause a renewed fellowship with sinners and outcasts, so his presence brings new meaning
to the piety practiced by John and Judaism. The presence of the bridegroom at the Messianic feast makes a
piety of gloom impossible. Fasting will be observed in
the church after Jesus' death, but, as 6:16–18 has already indicated, even then fasting must be done in a
festive manner.

The metaphor of "new wine in fresh wineskins" returns to Matthew's theme of continuity and change. If

the old order is willing to undergo radical conversion, then it will be saved. If not, then it will find the new wine of the kingdom unbearable (17). This plea for continuity and transformation will be sounded again in 13:52.

STUDY QUESTION: The Gospels never attempt to downplay the cost of discipleship. Following Jesus demands commitment and sacrifice. How costly is our own brand of discipleship?

FAITH IN JESUS' POWER OVER SICKNESS AND DEATH

18 While he was speaking to them, up came one of the officials, who bowed low in front of him and said, "My daughter had just died, but come and lay your hand on her and her life will be 19 saved." ·Jesus rose and, with his disciples, followed him.

20 Then from behind him came a woman, who had suffered from a hemorrhage for twelve years, 21 and she touched the fringe of his cloak, ·for she said to herself, "If I can only touch his cloak I 22 shall be well again." ·Jesus turned around and saw her and he said to her, "Courage, my daughter, your faith has restored you to health." And from that moment the woman was well again.

23 When Jesus reached the official's house and saw the flute players, with the crowd making a com- 24 motion he said, ·"Get out of here; the little girl is not dead, she is asleep." And they laughed at 25 him. ·But when the people had been turned out he went inside and took the little girl by the hand; 26 and she stood up. ·And the news spread all around the countryside.

27 As Jesus went on his way two blind men followed him shouting, "Take pity on us, Son of 28 David." ·And when Jesus reached the house the blind men came up with him and he said to them, "Do you believe I can do this?" They said, "Sir,

29 we do." ·Then he touched their eyes saying,
"Your faith deserves it, so let this be done for
30 you." ·And their sight returned. Then Jesus sternly
warned them, "Take care that no one learns
31 about this." ·But when they had gone, they talked
about him all over the countryside.
32   They had only just left when a man was brought
33 to him, a dumb demoniac. ·And when the devil
was cast out, the dumb man spoke and the people
were amazed. "Nothing like this has ever been in
34 Israel," they said. ·But the Pharisees said, "It is
through the prince of devils that he casts out
devils."
35   Jesus made a tour through all the towns and
villages, teaching in their synagogues, proclaiming
the Good News of the kingdom and curing all
kinds of diseases and sickness.

☩

The final segment of the miracle section seems to
concentrate on the question of faith. All the Gospels
stress the role of faith in Jesus' ministry of healing. The
miracles were not considered random flexes of divine
muscle, but vivid and effective signs of God's power to
restore humanity's wholeness. It was not just one's
sightless eyes or twisted limbs that needed restoration.
The most searing wound is in the human heart. True
healing would come when one responded by turning
one's whole self toward God. Thus if faith was not present, miracle was meaningless.

Matthew affirms this basic gospel notion through his
editing of the miracle stories. The official trusts in
Jesus' power to heal his daughter, even though she is
already dead (contrast Mk 5:23). The woman with
a hemorrhage is cured because her "faith has restored [her] to health" (22). (In Mark's version

[5:25–34] the reaction of the disciples and the presence of the crowd complicate the story, and the woman
experiences healing *before* she confesses her faith.
Matthew reverses the sequence in order to stress her
faith.) The two blind men (27–31) are able to see because their "faith deserves it."

The cure of the mute, which concludes the miracle
section, is hardly a miracle story at all, but merely a
peg on which to hang the contrasting reactions of the
crowd and the Pharisees (33–34). Here is the evangelist's prime concern: How does one respond to Jesus?
The people are in awe at Jesus' works of mercy just as
they were at his graceful words (7:29). But the Pharisees interpret Jesus' ministry as the work of Satan, not
the work of God. Their reaction is one more muffled
percussion which alerts the reader to the open rejection
of Jesus that will soon explode.

STUDY QUESTION: Jesus was not a magician. Healing
came only if the sick opened their
entire person to God's saving
power. Do we ask God for instant
magic or for the transforming miracle of faith?

Matthew 9:36 to 10:42
THE DISCIPLES AND JESUS' MISSION

Chapter 10 will bring us to the second great discourse of Matthew's Gospel, Jesus' mission instruction to his twelve disciples. One should not expect a neat, logical flow in this "discourse." As with the Sermon on the Mount, Matthew is content with a loose blend of materials from the sayings source and from Mark, tied together by his own reflections and conclusion.

36 And when he saw the crowds he felt sorry for them because they were harassed and dejected, like 37 sheep without a shepherd. ·Then he said to his disciples, "The harvest is rich but the laborers 38 are few, ·so ask the Lord of the harvest to send laborers to his harvest."

1 10 He summoned his twelve disciples, and gave them authority over unclean spirits with power to cast them out and to cure all kinds of diseases and sickness.
2 These are the names of the twelve apostles: first, Simon who is called Peter, and his brother Andrew; James the son of Zebedee, and his 3 brother John; ·Philip and Bartholomew; Thomas, and Matthew the tax collector; James the son of 4 Alphaeus, and Thaddaeus; ·Simon the Zealot and Judas Iscariot, the one who was to betray him.

✠

The preparation for Jesus' mission discourse recalls the scene preceding the Sermon on the Mount (see 4:23–25). Jesus is moved to speak because of his compassion for the fractured humanity that encircles him. Matthew employs two traditional images to set the tone. The people are confused and dejected, like "shepherdless sheep" (on this Old Testament image, see Ezk 34:3ff.; Jr 50:6). And they are expectant, like a "field of grain ready for the harvest," Jesus' own favored metaphor (cf. the parable of the sower, 13:4–9 and of the darnel, 13:24–30). But the mission of the gospel is no mere response to need; it is a gift from God. Therefore the Father must be asked to send the harvesters (38). The Beatitudes had asserted God's initiative at the beginning of the Sermon on the Mount, just as Jesus' call to prayer does here.

Matthew formalizes the call of the twelve disciples who will be "sent" on mission (thus earning the technical term "apostle," or "one sent forth"). The number is significant, because it is the number of the original twelve tribes of Israel. This confirms Matthew's insistence that Jesus' initial mission is to restore God's chosen people (10:5–6). The men Jesus chooses, themselves deserve the label "lost sheep": the awkward and fearful Peter; Matthew the tax collector; Simon, probably a member of the hot-blooded Zealot revolutionaries; and the tragic Judas. The gospel will be proclaimed by the very ones who desperately need it.

⁵ These twelve Jesus sent out, instructing them as follows:

"Do not turn your steps to pagan territory, and ⁶ do not enter any Samaritan town; •go rather to ⁷ the lost sheep of the House of Israel. •And as you go, proclaim that the kingdom of heaven is close ⁸ at hand. •Cure the sick, raise the dead, cleanse the lepers, cast out devils. You received without ⁹ charge, give without charge. •Provide yourselves with no gold or silver, not even with a few cop- ¹⁰ pers for your purses, •with no haversack for the journey or spare tunic or footwear or a staff, for the workman deserves his keep.

¹¹ "Whatever town or village you go into, ask for someone trustworthy and stay with him until you ¹²₁₃ leave. •As you enter his house, salute it, •and if the house deserves it, let your peace descend upon it; if it does not, let your peace come back to you. ¹⁴ And if anyone does not welcome you or listen to what you have to say, as you walk out of the ¹⁵ house or town shake the dust from your feet. •I tell you solemnly, on the day of Judgment it will not go as hard with the land of Sodom and Gomorrah as with that town.

✠

This instruction details the identity between Jesus' own ministry and that of the Twelve. They are to go only to the "lost sheep" of Israel. They are to proclaim the dawn of the kingdom (4:17). They are to continue the same works of compassion and reconciliation.

Some of the practical charges given probably reflect the style of the early gospel preachers. Like Jesus himself (cf. 8:20), the missionary is to travel light and is not to expect a salary for his work (8). He is to depend on the hospitality of Christian households as he moves from town to town. An underlying supposition of the discourse, and of other passages in Matthew (cf. 25:31ff.), is that preaching the gospel is a sacred task. The missionary becomes the voice and presence of Jesus himself (cf. 10:40). Therefore, welcoming or rejecting a missionary bears the same promise and the same consequence as welcoming or rejecting Jesus (14–15).

There is one intriguing omission in the list of mission tasks shared between Jesus and the disciples. Despite its centrality in Matthew's portrait of Jesus, "teaching" is not listed among the apostles' charges. That seems reserved to the very end of the Gospel (28:19–20), where the eleven apostles are given their commission to go to the whole world. Does Matthew want to imply that the disciples are not yet ready to "teach," because they have not yet confronted Jesus' Passion and death?

WARNING

¹⁶ Remember, I am sending you out like sheep among wolves; so be cunning as serpents and yet as harmless as doves.

¹⁷ "Beware of men: they will hand you over to Sanhedrins and scourge you in their synagogues.
¹⁸ You will be dragged before governors and kings for my sake, to bear witness before them and the
¹⁹ pagans. ·But when they hand you over, do not worry about how to speak or what to say; what you are to say will be given to you when the time
²⁰ comes: ·because it is not you who will be speaking; the Spirit of your Father will be speaking in you.

²¹ "Brother will betray brother to death, and the father his child; children will rise against their
²² parents and have them put to death. ·You will be hated by all men on account of my name; but the man who stands firm to the end will be saved.
²³ If they persecute you in one town, take refuge in the next; and if they persecute you in that, take refuge in another. I tell you solemnly, you will not have gone the round of the towns of Israel before the Son of Man comes.

²⁴ "The disciple is not superior to his teacher, nor
²⁵ the slave to his master. ·It is enough for the disciple that he should grow to be like his teacher,

and the slave like his master. If they have called
the master of the house Beelzebul, what will they
not say of his household?

✠

The discourse now runs sober. Jesus' own fate
warned the church that following him would be costly.
The Gospel's coursing life is a direct challenge to the
forces of death. So the disciple is warned to be open-
eyed and prudent (16).

Most of this section is taken from the apocalyptic
discourse of Mark's Gospel (see 13:9–13), where
Jesus' prophetic words alert the community to the turmoil it must expect in the last days. In Matthew these
same words are used in the mission discourse to help
express the kind of wrenching experiences the early
church has already had, and can continue to expect, as
it carries out its mission. Persecution, rejection, family
division: these are sometimes the cost of preaching the
gospel with integrity.

But pain is not the only sensation. Preaching the
gospel is ultimately to savor the joy and confidence
Jesus himself experienced. The Spirit of the Father will
give the disciples eloquence (20), and their task will
end with the "Son of Man's" victorious return (23).
This latter promise is difficult to interpret. The original
intent of the saying may reflect primitive Christianity's
hope that Jesus' victorious return was close at hand.
But for Matthew's own church, "the towns of Israel"
must now be understood as the far-flung villages of the
world to which the risen Lord has sent them (28:19).

Matthew 10:26–33
ENCOURAGEMENT

26 "Do not be afraid of them therefore. For everything that is now covered will be uncovered, and
27 everything now hidden will be made clear. ·What I say to you in the dark, tell in the daylight; what you hear in whispers, proclaim from the housetops.
28 "Do not be afraid of those who kill the body but cannot kill the soul; fear him rather who can de-
29 stroy both body and soul in hell. ·Can you not buy two sparrows for a penny? And yet not one falls to the ground without your Father knowing.
30 Why, every hair on your head has been counted.
31 So there is no need to be afraid; you are worth more than hundreds of sparrows.
32 "So if anyone declares himself for me in the presence of men, I will declare myself for him in
33 the presence of my Father in heaven. ·But the one who disowns me in the presence of men, I will disown in the presence of my Father in heaven.

✠

The hints of confidence in the previous section (see 19–20, 23) now break into full view. A series of metaphors not unlike the tone of the famous parable of the mustard seed (see 13:31–32) challenges the disciples to transmit the teaching of Jesus out loud and in the open (26–27). Paralyzing fear should not be an ingredient of Christian ministry. There is only one "fear" that should command a disciple, and that is fear of the One who holds the power of life in his hands (28). But such is not fear at all, but a consuming reverence and love for the Father, whose providence carefully watches over these more-precious-than-sparrows disciples (31).

Reference to the Father is now capped by reference to the Son, who reveals him to the disciples (32–33). Fearlessly proclaiming the gospel means fearlessly proclaiming Jesus. To fail at this is to snap off one's access to the Father.

Matthew 10:34–42
THE COSTLY BUSINESS OF
BEING A DISCIPLE

34 "Do not suppose that I have come to bring peace to the earth: it is not peace I have come to
35 bring, but a sword. ·For I have come to set a man against his father, a daughter against her mother, a daughter-in-law against her mother-in-
36 law. ·A man's enemies will be those of his own household.

37 "Anyone who prefers father or mother to me is not worthy of me. Anyone who prefers son or
38 daughter to me is not worthy of me. ·Anyone who does not take his cross and follow in my
39 footsteps is not worthy of me. ·Anyone who finds his life will lose it; anyone who loses his life for my sake will find it.

40 "Anyone who welcomes you welcomes me; and those who welcome me welcome the one who sent me.

41 "Anyone who welcomes a prophet because he is a prophet will have a prophet's reward; and anyone who welcomes a holy man because he is a holy man will have a holy man's reward.

42 "If anyone gives so much as a cup of cold water to one of these little ones because he is a disciple, then I tell you solemnly, he will most certainly not lose his reward."

✠

This discourse closes by lingering over the basic premise that began it. To preach the gospel is to be identified with Jesus. The Messiah was expected to bring "peace," but Jesus' jolting words deflate any hope for a cheap or superficial peace (34). Words taken from the prophet Micah (7:6) warn of family division (35–36). No allegiance can be allowed to shunt aside the gospel and the Jesus it proclaims (37–38). Such commitment is not blind fanaticism, but the discovery of life itself (39).

The final words of the discourse revert to the theme of hospitality. One who preaches the gospel, whose life is genuinely identified with that of Jesus, has become a sacred presence. This sacredness might be masked by the weakness, the half-faith, the fear, that Jesus' own disciples carry with them. But even a cup of water to one of these "little ones" (42) will not go unrewarded (cf. 25:31ff.).

STUDY QUESTION: The mission discourse pulls no punches: anyone who preaches the gospel with integrity will experience pain and joy. The discourse is directed to *all* who read the gospel, not just a select few. How do I preach the gospel? And in what ways do I experience the things Jesus speaks of in this instruction to his disciples?

*"Are You the One Who Is to Come,
or Have We Got to Wait for Someone Else?"
Reactions to Jesus and His Message*
Matthew 11:1 to 16:20

Matthew 11:1–15
"ARE YOU THE ONE?"

¹ 11 When Jesus had finished instructing his twelve disciples he moved on from there to teach and preach in their towns.

² Now John in his prison had heard what Christ was doing and he sent his disciples to ask him, ³ "Are you the one who is to come, or have we got ⁴ to wait for someone else?" ·Jesus answered, "Go ⁵ back and tell John what you hear and see; ·the blind see again, and the lame walk, lepers are cleansed, and the deaf hear, and the dead are raised to life and the Good News is proclaimed ⁶ to the poor; ·and happy is the man who does not lose faith in me."

⁷ As the messengers were leaving, Jesus began to talk to the people about John: "What did you go out into the wilderness to see? A reed swaying in ⁸ the breeze? No? ·Then what did you go out to see? A man wearing fine clothes? Oh no, those who wear fine clothes are to be found in palaces. ⁹ Then what did you go out for? To see a prophet? Yes, I tell you, and much more than a prophet: ¹⁰ he is the one of whom scripture says:

Look, I am going to send my messenger before you;
he will prepare your way before you.

11   "I tell you solemnly, of all the children born of
      women, a greater than John the Baptist has never
      been seen: yet the least in the kingdom of heaven
12   is greather than he is. •Since John the Baptist
      came, up to this present time, the kingdom of
      heaven has been subjected to violence and the
13   violent are taking it by storm. •Because it was
      toward John that all the prophecies of the proph-
14   ets and of the Law were leading; •and he, if you
      will believe me, is the Elijah who was to return.
15   If anyone has ears to hear, let him listen!

✠

Matthew's transitional formula (cf. above 7:28–29)
signals a major turning point in the Gospel. Matthew
has laid before us a portrait of Jesus, the Son of God,
the Messiah of graceful word (Chs. 5–7) and healing
touch (Chs. 8–9). Chapter 10 has claimed that Jesus'
disciples and, through them, the church are to carry
out the same mission. How will people respond? This
question will dominate Chapters 11 to 13, and its consequences will be played out in the rest of the gospel
story.

The figure of John the Baptist prefaced Matthew's
account of the ministry of Jesus (3:1–15); now response to the gospel will once more bind their fates together. A question of John's disciples enunciates the
theme of the entire section: "Are you the one who is to
come, or have we got to wait for someone else?" (3).
Jesus' answer (4–5) uses the prophetic words of Isaiah
(cf. 61:1; 35:5f.) to tick off the preaching and healing
ministry described in the previous chapters of the Gospel. Jesus is the expected Messiah, the "one who is to
come." And as Matthew's additions to the words of
Isaiah suggest ("lepers are cleansed . . . the dead are

raised to life"), Jesus is more than Israel expected. A new Beatitude reasserts the chapter's theme: happy is the one who does not find Jesus an obstacle (6).

The contrast between John and Jesus is instructive (7–15). What did the people think of the desert prophet John? He was more than a prophet, because he announced the arrival of Jesus. John is "Elijah," the great prophet hero of the Old Testament, who was expected to reappear immediately before the Messianic age (cf. Si 48:10; Ml 3:23). But John, for all his greatness, is still subordinate to Jesus. John represented the best of Israel; Jesus is the beginning of a new age. The saying about "violence" is obscure (12), but it seems to capture the dramatic rush of life triggered by Jesus' arrival. The kingdom of God is being taken by storm, because God's Son has brought the kingdom into the dusty squares of Galilee.

STUDY QUESTION: John's mysterious figure continues to haunt the Gospel story. His presence and his words prepare for Jesus' coming, but John does not get in Jesus' way. We might consider the figure of John as a model of Christian ministry.

THIS GENERATION'S FAILURE

16   "What description can I find for this generation? It is like children shouting to each other as they sit in the market place:

17
> 'We played the pipes for you,
> and you wouldn't dance;
> we sang dirges,
> and you wouldn't be mourners.'

18 "For John came, neither eating nor drinking, and
19 they say, 'He is possessed.' ·The Son of Man came, eating and drinking, and they say, "Look, a glutton and a drunkard, a friend of tax collectors and sinners.' Yet wisdom has been proved right by her actions."
20   Then he began to reproach the towns in which most of his miracles had been worked, because they refused to repent.
21   "Alas for you, Chorazin! Alas for you, Bethsaida! For if the miracles done in you had been in Tyre and Sidon, they would have repented long
22 ago in sackcloth and ashes. ·And still, I tell you that it will not go as hard on Judgment day with
23 Tyre and Sidon as with you. ·And as for you, Capernaum, did you want to be exalted as high as heaven? You shall be thrown down to hell. For if the miracles done in you had been done in

²⁴ Sodom, it would have been standing yet. •And
still, I tell you that it will not go as hard with the
land of Sodom on Judgment day as with you."

✠

The Gospel has yet to describe the hostile resistance
that will be thrown against Jesus and his message. But
this passage is well aware of what lies ahead. "This
generation"—indicative not only of Jesus' contemporaries but of the opponents of Matthew's own community—rejects John's prophetic message of repentance and Jesus' joyous ministry of the kingdom. The
tragedy of Jesus' words is barely masked by an almost
humorous comparison to the children of the market
place who imitate the men who play the pipes at a
wedding and the women who mourn at a funeral
(16–17). The leaders of his own people will not join
him. Their contemptuous label ironically confirms the
Gospel's portrayal of Jesus' sensitive rapport with the
outcasts: "a glutton and a drunkard, a friend of tax
collectors and sinners." Yet the works Jesus does (see
v. 1) are truly the works of wisdom (19). Jesus' compassion proves that he is the Son of his Father. This
theme will re-emerge at the end of the chapter (see
11:25–30).
One of Matthew's most insistent messages is that
confrontation with Jesus and the gospel bears its own
responsibility. To reject the gospel or to fail to take it
seriously through repentance and good deeds is to invite judgment. The Galilean towns where Jesus will
suffer rejection are promised such consequences:
Chorazin, Bethsaida, Capernaum. This is Jesus' home
region clustered around the lake, but such proximity to

Jesus is meaningless unless one takes his message to heart.

STUDY QUESTION: Jesus and his message cannot be toyed with. To hear the gospel brings responsibility. What difference has the gospel made in our lives, we who have heard it so often?

Matthew 11:25–30
"THE CHILDREN WHO SEE"

25 At that time Jesus exclaimed, "I bless you, Father, Lord of heaven and of earth, for hiding these things from the learned and the clever and
26 revealing them to mere children. ·Yes, Father, for
27 that is what it pleased you to do. ·Everything has been entrusted to me by my Father; and no one knows the Son except the Father, just as no one knows the Father except the Son and those to whom the Son chooses to reveal him.

28 "Come to me, all you who labor and are over-
29 burdened, and I will give you rest. ·Shoulder my yoke and learn from me, for I am gentle and humble in heart, and you will find rest for your
30 souls. ·Yes, my yoke is easy and my burden light."

⊬

Acceptance or rejection of Jesus and his message is crucial because of who he is. These verses, which are supremely important in Matthew's Gospel, assert Jesus' identity in unmistakable terms.

The passage begins with a "thanksgiving," a prayer form common in Judaism and in early-Christian liturgy. The lyrical cadence of the prayer and its emphasis on revelation causes many commentators to note its similarity to the style of John's Gospel. But these verses are completely at home in Matthew. Jesus' bond with his Father has been stressed from the beginning of the Gospel. The obedient Jesus is God's Son; not just *a* son, but *the* Son, whose very presence is God's last and best word to Israel (27). The context of this chapter and the wider framework of the Gospel will prove that the learned and self-righteous are blind to the beauty of the gospel, while the outcasts and sinners—"mere children"—respond with faith.

Themes of intimate revelation to a chosen few and the Son's privileged knowledge of his Father are found in the early chapters of The Book of Wisdom (see, e.g., 2:13, 17–18). Ecclesiasticus (see 51:23–27; 24:19, 26), another Old Testament wisdom book, also seems to be an influence on the beautiful words that conclude the chapter (28–30). The compassion of Jesus invites the weary and burdened to come to find rest. In Ecclesiasticus, the Jewish Law is personified and offers an almost identical invitation to those who seek God's will. Jesus is God's new "law." His "yoke" (another Jewish image for obedience to the Law) is easy to those who accept it. His burden is no oppressive network of legal prescriptions, but the joy of a single call to love.

STUDY QUESTION: Matthew portrays Jesus as the ulti- mate revelation of who God is. Does our own image of God har- monize with the compassionate and forgiving God that Jesus reveals?

Matthew 12:1–21
THE PRICE OF COMPASSION

1 **12** At that time Jesus took a walk one sabbath day through the cornfields. His disciples were hungry and began to pick ears of corn and
2 eat them. ·The Pharisees noticed it and said to him, "Look, your disciples are doing something
3 that is forbidden on the sabbath." ·But he said to them, "Have you not read what David did when he
4 and his followers were hungry—·how he went into the house of God and how they ate the loaves of offering which neither he nor his followers were allowed to eat, but which were for the priests
5 alone? ·Or again, have you not read in the Law that on the sabbath day the Temple priests break
6 the sabbath without being blamed for it? ·Now here, I tell you, is something greater than the
7 Temple. ·And if you had understood the meaning of the words: What I want is mercy, not sacrifice, you would not have condemned the blameless.
8 For the Son of Man is master of the sabbath."
9 He moved on from there and went to their
10 synagogue, ·and a man was there at the time who had a withered hand. They asked him, "Is it against the law to cure a man on the sabbath day?" hoping for something to use against him.
11 But he said to them, "If any one of you here had only one sheep and it fell down a hole on the sabbath day, would he not get hold of it

12 and lift it out? ·Now a man is far more important
than a sheep, so it follows that it is permitted
13 to do good on the sabbath day." ·Then he said to
the man, "Stretch out your hand." He stretched
it out and his hand was better, as sound as the
14 other one. ·At this the Pharisees went out and
began to plot against him, discussing how to destroy him.
15   Jesus knew this and withdrew from the district.
16 Many followed him and he cured them all, ·but
17 warned them not to make him known. ·This was
to fulfill the prophecy of Isaiah:

18   Here is my servant whom I have chosen,
      my beloved, the favorite of my soul.
      I will endow him with my spirit,
      and he will proclaim the true faith to the nations.
19   He will not brawl or shout,
      nor will anyone hear his voice in the streets.
20   He will not break the crushed reed,
      nor put out the smoldering wick
      till he had led the truth to victory:
21   in his name the nations will put their hope.

☩

The teaching of Jesus is an easy yoke and a light burden because his words and his ministry center on compassion and love. This was the final note of Chapter
11. The two Sabbath incidents that begin Chapter 12
are examples of Jesus' teaching in action.

Deuteronomy 23:25 forbade "reaping" on the Sabbath, part of the many laws that were intended to
picket off the sacred day of rest. Thus the Pharisees
object when Jesus' disciples pick ears of corn
(12:1–2). As Matthew presents the story, Jesus de-
fends his disciples because they are hungry. Thus the
Sabbath law should be interpreted in the light of this

clear human need. Two examples, one from history and one from the Law itself, back up Jesus' interpretation. David looked after the needs of his own followers at the expense of the law (see 1 S 21:4–7) and the priests themselves have to bend some of the Sabbath legislation in order to carry out their liturgical duties in the Temple (see Nb 28:9–10). But the final argument is Jesus' own authority (12:8). The primacy of compassion and mercy over all the other demands of the Law is at the heart of Jesus' definitive revelation of the Father's will. The words of Hosea 6:6 (see v. 7) are once again cited as an exquisite summary of Jesus' teaching (see 9:13).

Another Sabbath incident (9–14) continues the illustration of Jesus' priorities. The hostility that now smolders between Jesus and his opponents is scarcely veiled. As Matthew notes (9), Jesus goes to *"their* synagogue" and the question put to him is meant to be a trap: "Is it against the law to cure a man on the sabbath day?" Jesus' interpretation is fearlessly proclaimed by word and action. Can one rescue an entrapped sheep on the Sabbath (a point that was, in fact, hotly debated by the rabbis)? If one can show compassion to an animal, how much more should the deliverance of a human person become an urgent priority. Jesus' healing of the man with the withered hand is the final word. What Jesus teaches, he does; this has been the constant insistence of Matthew's Gospel (cf. 7:24). The Pharisees' hostility, which will eventually boil into total rejection of Jesus, begins now (14).

Because of the leaders' opposition, Jesus "withdraws from the district." A brief summary informs us that he quietly continues his ministry of compassion (15). The words of Isaiah 42:1–4, thoroughly adapted to fit the evangelist's purpose, provide an interlude of quiet reflection on the significance of Jesus and his ministry as the din of opposition begins to build. Jesus is God's faithful "servant," and in words reminiscent of the baptism (cf. 3:17), he is the beloved and spirit-filled Son of God. The Greek word *pais* can mean servant or child (son), and Matthew may intend both senses here. His ministry is not a brawling display of power, a conception of Messiahship Jesus rejected out of hand in the desert (see 4:1–11). This gentle, selfless Servant comes to bring a decisive moment of judgment to his own people and to be a sign of hope to the "nations."

STUDY QUESTION: Jesus is a model of integrity: what he teaches, he does. He carries out his mission resolutely and without fanfare. Sometimes our own good deeds are done with a side glance toward the approving crowd.

WHAT KIND OF SPIRIT

22 Then they brought to him a blind and dumb
demoniac; and he cured him, so that the dumb
23 man could speak and see. ·All the people were
astounded and said, "Can this be the Son of
24 David?" ·But when the Pharisees heard this they
said, "The man casts out devils only through
Beelzebul, the prince of devils."

25 Knowing what was in their minds he said to
them, "Every kingdom divided against itself is
heading for ruin; and no town, no household
26 divided against itself can stand. ·Now if Satan
casts out Satan, he is divided against himself; so
27 how can his kingdom stand? ·And if it is through
Beelzebul that I cast out devils, through whom
do your own experts cast them out? Let them be
28 your judges, then. ·But if it is through the Spirit
of God that I cast devils out, then know that the
kingdom of God has overtaken you.

29 "Or again, how can anyone make his way into
a strong man's house and burgle his property unless he has tied up the strong man first? Only
then can he burgle his house.

30 "He who is not with me is against me, and he
31 who does not gather with me scatters. ·And so I
tell you, every one of men's sins and blasphemies
will be forgiven, but blasphemy against the Spirit
32 will not be forgiven. ·And anyone who says a
word against the Son of Man will be forgiven;

but let anyone speak against the Holy Spirit and
he will not be forgiven either in this world or in
the next.

33   "Make a tree sound and its fruit will be sound;
make a tree rotten and its fruit will be rotten. For
34 the tree can be told by its fruit. ·Brood of vipers,
how can your speech be good when you are evil?
For a man's words flow out of what fills his
35 heart. ·A good man draws good things from his
store of goodness; a bad man draws bad things
36 from his store of badness. ·So I tell you this, that
for every unfounded word men utter they will an-
37 swer on Judgment day, ·since it is by your words
you will be acquitted, and by your words condemned."

38   Then some of the scribes and Pharisees spoke
up. "Master," they said, "we should like to see
39 a sign from you." ·He replied, "It is an evil and
unfaithful generation that asks for a sign! The
only sign it will be given is the sign of the prophet
40 Jonah. ·For as Jonah was in the belly of the sea
monster for three days and three nights, so will
the Son of Man be in the heart of the earth for
41 three days and three nights. ·On Judgment day
the men of Nineveh will stand up with this generation and condemn it, because when Jonah
preached they repented; and there is something
42 greater than Jonah here. ·On Judgment day the
Queen of the South will rise up with this generation and condemn it, because she came from the
ends of the earth to hear the wisdom of Solomon;
and there is something greater than Solomon
here.

43   "When an unclean spirit goes out of a man it
wanders through waterless country looking for a
44 place to rest, and cannot find one. ·Then it says,
'I will return to the home I came from.' But on
arrival, finding it unoccupied, swept and tidied,
45 it then goes off and collects seven other spirits
more evil than itself, and they go in and set up
house there, so that the man ends up by being

worse than he was before. That is what will happen to this evil generation."

46 He was still speaking to the crowds when his mother and his brothers appeared; they were standing outside and were anxious to have a word
48 with him. ·But to the man who told him this Jesus replied, Who is my mother? Who are my broth-
49 ers?" ·And stretching out his hand toward his disciples he said, "Here are my mother and my
50 brothers. ·Anyone who does the will of my Father in heaven, he is my brother and sister and mother."

☩

Matthew moves back to the theme of responsibility which dominates these chapters. An exorcism triggers contrasting reactions (22–24). The crowd is astounded and edges to the brink of recognizing Jesus: "Can this be the Son of David?" This Messianic title was given to Jesus in the first verse of the Gospel (see 1:1). But the Pharisees judge that Jesus' power is not from God but from "the prince of devils."

Exorcisms pose in stark terms the ultimate significance of the gospel. The power of God at work in Jesus' teaching and healing overwhelms the forces of darkness and death. For this reason Matthew gives considerable attention to the Pharisees' accusation. Apparently playing on the popular etymology for the name "Beelzebul" as "Lord of the House," Jesus asks how Satan's household could be so divided that Jesus' actions, which in fact destroy Satan's kingdom, can be construed as acting on behalf of Satan. Jesus' conclusion is inevitable and awesome: if Jesus acts through the power of God—as the Gospel testifies he does— then the longed-for reign of God has already begun to

make its presence felt (28). A "mini-parable" restates
Jesus' case in novel terms. Jesus is a "thief" who
breaks into Satan's household, ties up that "strong
man," and plunders his property (29).

The stark cleavage between the Gospel's estimation
of Jesus and the Pharisees' characterization of him as
in league with Beelzebul forces a decision: one is either
for or against Jesus (30). In the difficult verses 31–32,
the theme of response and the image of Jesus as Spirit-
filled messenger (cf. the quote from Isaiah in verse 18)
seem to converge. Ignorance might excuse one who
rejects Jesus, the Son of Man. But to reject the Spirit of
God which animates Jesus is equivalent to rejecting
God himself and is therefore unforgivable. To reject
forgiveness is to effectively place oneself in unpardona-
ble circumstances.

A series of sayings continue Matthew's sober commentary on the rejection of Jesus (33–37). The familiar image of a tree and its fruits (cf. 7:16–20) is used
again to illustrate the continuity between good deeds
and a good heart, between bad deeds and an evil heart.
The significant things we say or do have consequences
because they reveal the basic values commanding our
lives.

The chapter draws to a close with another gallery of
contrasting attitudes. The scribes and Pharisees continue to reject Jesus by demanding a sign, thereby im-
plying that the testimony of his own teaching and ministry is insufficient (38–45). Those who accept Jesus
and thus have true kinship with him are his disciples,
who do the will of his Father (46–50).

The demand for some clinching guarantee that Jesus
is the one will be honored only with the sign of Jonah,
a sign that turns out to be nothing other than Jesus'

own life and ministry. Verse 40, which refers to
Jonah's famous sojourn in the belly of the sea monster,
alludes to Jesus' death and resurrection. Verse 41 recalls Jonah's preaching to the pagan Ninevites. Jesus'
own mission is turned aside by Israel but is accepted as
a sign of hope by gentiles (cf. v. 21). This, too, should
be a warning for those who turn a deaf ear to someone
who is greater than Jonah and wiser than Solomon.

The pointed story of the return of the unclean spirit
adds another warning to the list (43–45). Jesus' ministry is a cleansing purge of Israel. But if there is no response to his mission, the evil that had been driven out
will come back to fill the void.

Early in the Gospel, John the Baptist warned that
descent from Abraham meant nothing unless it was
coupled with genuine repentance (3:9). A similar atmosphere surrounds the story that closes Chapter 12
(46–50). The family of Jesus has no claim on him. A
bond of kinship is forged with Jesus only when one
shares his dominating drive to do the will of his Father
in heaven.

STUDY QUESTION: What do we perceive in Jesus? And
what difference does our perception
make in our lives? These are the
probing questions Matthew's Gospel continues to hurl at the reader.

Matthew 13:1–58
MANY THINGS IN PARABLES

13:1–3 INTRODUCTION

13 ¹ ² That same day, Jesus left the house and sat by the lakeside, ·but such crowds gathered around him that he got into a boat and sat there. ³ The people all stood on the beach, ·and he told them many things in parables.

✠

The third great discourse of Matthew's Gospel now begins. Like the previous two (cf. the Sermon of Chapters 5–7 and the mission discourse of Chapter 10), this "discourse" is really a composite of Jesus' words brought together by the evangelist from his various sources and designed to emphasize major themes of the Gospel.

We instinctively think of the parables as those pointed, colorful stories Jesus told in order to communicate with his audience. But Matthew views the parables from another perspective. As Chapters 11 and 12 have demonstrated, some people were open to Jesus' teaching, but others closed their minds and hearts to the gospel. For this latter group the parables are not provocative bearers of truth but puzzling riddles they refuse to understand. The Hebrew word for parable, *mashal*, was wide enough to contain both nuances: explanatory metaphor and baffling riddle. In Matthew's Gospel, Jesus' teaching becomes "parable," an opaque riddle for those who refuse to understand, but revelation of the mystery of the kingdom for his disciples. Thus the theme of response to Jesus that dominated Chapters 11 and 12 is kept alive.

The evangelist has impressed a loose structure on this composite discourse. The first section (1–23) is dominated by a cleavage between the disciples, who do understand, and the crowds, who do not. The second section of the discourse (24–50) is concerned with the judgment that will separate the sons of the kingdom from the sons of evil. Most of the material in the first section is adapted from Mark; most of the material in the second is unique to Matthew. And both sections are dominated by a similar pattern: introductory parables to the crowds, comment on the reason for speaking in parables, and finally, private instruction for the disciples.

Matthew 13:4–23
ON BEING A DISCIPLE OR BEING PART
OF THE CROWD

4   He said, "Imagine a sower going out to sow. ·As
he sowed, some seeds fell on the edge of the path,
5 and the birds came and ate them up. ·Others fell
on patches of rock where they found little soil
and sprang up straight away, because there was
6 no depth of earth; ·but as soon as the sun came
up they were scorched and, not having any roots,
7 they withered away. ·Others fell among thorns,
8 and the thorns grew up and choked them. ·Others
fell on rich soil and produced their crop, some
9 a hundredfold, some sixty, some thirty. ·Listen,
anyone who has ears·"

10   Then the disciples went up to him and asked,
11 "Why do you talk to them in parables?" ·Be-
cause," he replied, "the mysteries of the kingdom
of heaven are revealed to you, but they are not
12 revealed to them. ·For anyone who has will be
given more, and he will have more than enough;
but from anyone who has not, even what he has
13 will be taken away. ·The reason I talk to them
in parables is that they look without seeing and
14 listen without hearing or understanding ·So in
their case this prophecy of Isaiah is being fulfilled:

You will listen and listen again, but not
   understand,
see and see again, but not perceive.

15 For the heart of this nation has grown coarse,
their ears are dull of hearing, and they have
    shut their eyes.
for fear they should see with their eyes,
hear with their ears,
understand with their heart,
and be converted
and be healed by me.

16 "But happy are your eyes because they see,
17 your ears because they hear! ·I tell you solemnly,
many prophets and holy men longed to see what
you see, and never saw it; to hear what you hear,
and never heard it.
18 "You, therefore, are to hear the parable of the
19 sower. ·When anyone hears the word of the kingdom without understanding, the evil one comes
and carries off what was sown in his heart: this
is the man who received the seed on the edge of
20 the path. ·The one who received it on patches of
rock is the man who hears the word and wel-
21 comes it at once with joy. ·But he has no root
in him, he does not last; let some trial come, or
some persecution on account of the word, and he
22 falls away at once. ·The one who received the
seed in thorns is the man who hears the word,
but the worries of this world and the lure of
riches choke the word and so he produces noth-
23 ing. ·And the one who received the seed in rich
soil is the man who hears the word and understands it; he is the one who yields a harvest and
produces now a hundredfold, now sixty, now
thirty."

✠

The parable of the sower (4–9) begins the discourse. By itself, the story of the seed and its fate on so
many kinds of soil seems to emphasize the inevitability
of a rich crop (some a hundredfold, some sixty, some

thirty) in spite of all obstacles. But the final phrase calling the listener to attention, and the explanation of the parable given by Jesus to his disciples (18–23), will shift the emphasis to the theme of *response*. This is where the focus of the chapter will remain.

Response is certainly the topic of the next segment (10–17), in which Jesus explains to the disciples his reason for speaking to the crowds in parables. The followers of Jesus were singled out at the end of Chapter 12 because they were dedicated to the will of the Father. Here they are cited for being open to understanding the mysteries of the kingdom of heaven revealed to them by Jesus. But for the crowds who have not yet committed themselves to Jesus and who eventually will turn against him (see 27:24–25), the teaching of Jesus is not revelation but "parable." Words adopted from Isaiah 6:9f. spell out the reasons for the indictment: "they look without seeing and listen without hearing or understanding" (13–14).

The first half of the discourse concludes with Jesus' explanation of the parable of the sower (18–23). The disciples *do hear* what Jesus says, and thus they can understand the point of the story of the sower. The early church loved to allegorize the parables of Jesus, and it is likely that Matthew uses this technique here in order to continue the discourse's concentration on the theme of response. The various fates of the seeds illustrate various reactions to the gospel. In some people the gospel takes no root at all, because they are "without understanding." Others begin well but soon allow persecution or the lust for wealth to choke off the new life in them. Verse 23 defines the genuine disciple: "the one who hears the word and understands it; he is the one who yields a harvest and produces now a hundred-fold, now sixty, now thirty."

STUDY QUESTION: This section's emphasis on perception and action, on hearing and doing, bears Matthew's unmistakable brand. For the evangelist there is no genuine faith unless it is translated into decisive action. Do we agree?

Matthew 13:24–58
ON BEING A SUBJECT OF THE KINGDOM
AND A SUBJECT OF THE EVIL ONE

[24] He put another parable before them, "The kingdom of heaven may be compared to a man [25] who sowed good seed in his field. ·While everybody was asleep his enemy came, sowed darnel [26] all among the wheat, and made off. ·When the new wheat sprouted and ripened, the darnel appeared as well. [27] ·The owner's servants went to him and said, 'Sir, was it not good seed that you sowed in your field? If so, where does the darnel [28] come from?' ·'Some enemy has done this,' he answered. And the servants said, 'Do you want us [29] to go and weed it out?' ·But he said, 'No, because when you weed out the darnel you might pull [30] up the wheat with it. ·Let them both grow till the harvest; and at harvest time I shall say to the reapers: First collect the darnel and tie it in bundles to be burned, then gather the wheat into my barn.' "

[31] He put another parable before them, "The kingdom of heaven is like a mustard seed which [32] a man took and sowed in his field. ·It is the smallest of all the seeds, but when it has grown it is the biggest shrub of all and becomes a tree so that the birds of the air come and shelter in its branches."

[33] He told them another parable, "The kingdom

of heaven is like the yeast a woman took and
mixed in with three measures of flour till it was
leavened all through."
³⁴ In all this Jesus spoke to the crowds in parables; indeed, he would never speak to them ex-
³⁵ cept in parables. ·This was to fulfill the prophecy:

I will speak to you in parables
and expound things hidden since the foundation
    of the world.

³⁶ Then, leaving the crowds, he went to the house;
and his disciples came to him and said, "Explain
the parable about the darnel in the field to us."
³⁷ He said in reply, "The sower of the good seed
³⁸ is the Son of Man. ·The field is the world; the
good seed is the subjects of the kingdom; the
³⁹ darnel, the subjects of the evil one; ·the enemy
who sowed them, the devil; the harvest is the end
⁴⁰ of the world; the reapers are the angels. ·Well
then, just as the darnel is gathered up and burned
⁴¹ in the fire, so it will be at the end of time. ·The
Son of Man will send his angels and they will
gather out of his kingdom all things that provoke
⁴² offenses and all who do evil, ·and throw them
into the blazing furnace, where there will be weep-
⁴³ ing and grinding of teeth. ·Then the virtuous
will shine like the sun in the kingdom of their Father. Listen, anyone who has ears!
⁴⁴ "The kingdom of heaven is like treasure hidden in a field which someone has found; he hides
it again, goes off happy, sells everything he owns
and buys the field.
⁴⁵ "Again, the kingdom of heaven is like a mer-
⁴⁶ chant looking for fine pearls; ·when he finds one
of great value he goes and sells everything he
owns and buys it.
⁴⁷ "Again, the kingdom of heaven is like a dragnet cast into the sea that brings in a haul of all
⁴⁸ kinds. ·When it is full, the fishermen haul it
ashore; then, sitting down, they collect the good

ones in a basket and throw away those that are
49 no use. ·This is how it will be at the end of time:
the angels will appear and separate the wicked
50 from the just ·to throw them into the blazing
furnace where there will be weeping and grinding of teeth.
51   "Have you understood all this?" They said,
52 "Yes." ·And he said to them, "Well then, every
scribe who becomes a disciple of the kingdom of
heaven is like a householder who brings out from
his storeroom things both new and old."
53   When Jesus had finished these parables he left
54 the district; ·and, coming to his home town, he
taught the people in their synagogue in such a
way that they were astonished and said, "Where
did the man get this wisdom and these miracu-
55 lous powers? ·This is the carpenter's son, surely?
Is not his mother the woman called Mary, and
his brothers James and Joseph and Simon and
56 Jude? ·His sisters, too, are they not all here with
57 us? So where did the man get it all?" ·And they
would not accept him. But Jesus said to them,
"A prophet is only despised in his own country
58 and in his own house," ·and he did not work
many miracles there because of their lack of
faith.

✠

The pattern of the first half of the discourse is
repeated. Parables to the crowds (24–33) will be followed by a comment on the reasons for parables
(34–35) and with private instructions to the disciples
(35–50). The cleavage between the disciples, who understand, and the crowds, who do not, dominated the
earlier material. The surrounding context of Chapters
11 and 12 leaves little doubt that this contrast is a
reflection on Israel's rejection of Jesus. But the broader

spectrum of images in the last half of the discourse (the "world," the "wicked," and the "just," etc.) indicates that Matthew is not confining the challenge of the discourse only to this problem. *All* who hear the gospel —Jew and gentile—must decide whether it will be riddle or revelation.

A string of parables is now directed to the crowds. The parable of the darnel will receive its allegorical explanation later on (see 36–43). The images of the mustard seed and the yeast (31–33) contrast unpretentious beginnings with glorious and powerful endings. They are a brisk warning to those who cannot perceive that in Jesus the kingdom is already at work (cf. 12:28).

A citation from Ps 78:2 (13:35) verifies the fact that Jesus' teaching in "parables" (i.e. riddles) and the rejection of his mission which this implies are all within the scope of God's plan prophesied in the Scriptures. Jesus now leaves the crowds outside and gathers his disciples inside a house (36). The movement is a commentary on the closed hearts of those who refuse to understand Jesus.

Practically every detail of the parable of the darnel receives an explanation (36–43). The story becomes symbolic of judgment, a favored theme of Matthew. Those in the world will be called to responsibility at the great harvest. Another assortment of judgment parables, all of them unique to Matthew's Gospel, will be found in Chapter 25.

The exquisite stories of the treasure in the field and the pearl merchant (44–46) play out the theme of responsibility in another key. Seeking the kingdom or, as Matthew puts it in other contexts, doing the will of the Father (12:50), calls for total commitment. One does not casually add this pearl to a collection or simply purchase one more parcel of land. *All* must be sold. An absolute fresh start is to be made.

The theme of judgment returns with the story of the dragnet (47–50). Its structure and message are practically identical to that of the darnel (cf. 24–30). The gospel cuts into one's life and one must decide. Jesus brings compassion and healing; he also brings a call to responsibility that is not without its consequences.

The parable discourse concludes as it had begun— with the theme of "understanding" (51–52). The disciples perceive the beauty and the truth of Jesus' words, and the Gospel will document their struggle to make that understanding bear fruit. The speech is concluded with a saying that practically defines the purpose of Matthew's Gospel. The scribe (i.e. one adept at the Law) who becomes a disciple of the kingdom is one who can bring from his storeroom "things both new and old." Jesus himself was such a "householder," fulfilling the past by transforming the present. His disciples had to do the same by discovering the promises of Israel's heritage in the challenge of Jesus' teaching.

Matthew's standard transitional formula (53) signals that the discourse is over and the tempo of the narrative will resume. The scene flashes to Jesus' hometown of Nazareth (54–58). His own people hear his words and witness his power, but they refuse to accept him. The chasm that separates Jesus and those who should have understood him recalls the scene at the end of Chapter 12 (v. 46–50). Kinship with Jesus cannot be presumed. The two stories pointedly frame Jesus' discourse on the urgency of "understanding."

STUDY QUESTION: Christians can sometimes speak too casually about "belonging to Christ" or of "following Jesus." But the parable discourse warns us that kinship with Jesus should not be lightly presumed. A disciple of Jesus is one who has pondered his words and translated them into his or her life.

PROPHETS WITHOUT HONOR

1 2 **14** At that time Herod the tetrarch heard about the reputation of Jesus, ·and said to his court, "This is John the Baptist himself; he has risen from the dead, and that is why miraculous powers are at work in him."

3 Now it was Herod who had arrested John, chained him up and put him in prison because of Herodias, his brother Philip's wife. 4 For John had told him, "It is against the Law 5 for you to have her." ·He had wanted to kill him but was afraid of the people, who regarded John 6 as a prophet. ·Then, during the celebrations for Herod's birthday, the daughter of Herodias danced before the company, and so delighted 7 Herod ·that he promised on oath to give her any- 8 thing she asked. ·Prompted by her mother she said, "Give me John the Baptist's head, here, on 9 a dish." ·The king was distressed but, thinking of the oaths he had sworn and of his guests, he 10 ordered it to be given her, ·and sent and had 11 John beheaded in the prison. ·The head was brought in on a dish and given to the girl who 12 took it to her mother. ·John's disciples came and took the body and buried it; then they went off to tell Jesus.

✠

Herod's interest in Jesus and his speculation that Jesus might be John the Baptist brought back from the dead (14:1–2) occasions a flashback. At the beginning of Jesus' public ministry (4:12), we were told that John had been arrested. Later on, the imprisoned prophet had sent messengers to Jesus (11:2). Now John's tragic story is completed. Herod Antipas, son of Herod the Great and vassal of the Romans over the region of Galilee and Perea, arrested John because the prophet had opposed Herod's incestuous marriage to Herodias, wife of his half brother. Because of a frivolous oath, Herod submits to his wife's instigations and kills the prophet (thereby providing a negative example, as Peter will do at the trial, of Jesus' prohibition against oath taking; cf. 5:33–37).

This flashback, and the warning transmitted to Jesus, bind John and Jesus together once again. At the beginning of Chapter 11, Jesus had challenged his contemporaries for their rejection of himself and John. Now John's death as a prophet forecasts Jesus' own fate (see verse 5; cf. 21:46, where the identical word is used of Jesus). The Gospel will speak openly of the Passion in Chapter 16 (see 16:21), but the end result of the mounting hostility against Jesus is already clear.

13 When Jesus received this news he withdrew by boat to a lonely place where they could be by themselves. But the people heard of this and, 14 leaving the towns, went after him on foot. ·So as he stepped ashore he saw a large crowd; and he took pity on them and healed their sick.

15 When evening came, the disciples went to him and said, "This is a lonely place, and the time has slipped by; so send the people away, and they can go to the villages to buy themselves some 16 food." ·Jesus replied, "There is no need for them to go: give them something to eat yourselves." 17 But they answered, "All we have with us is five 18 loaves and two fish." ·"Bring them here to me," 19 he said. ·He gave orders that the people were to sit down on the grass; then he took the five loaves and the two fish, raised his eyes to heaven and said the blessing. And breaking the loaves he handed them to his disciples who gave them to 20 the crowds. ·They all ate as much as they wanted, and they collected the scraps remaining, twelve 21 baskets full. ·Those who ate numbered about five thousand men, to say nothing of women and children.

22 Directly after this he made the disciples get into the boat and go on ahead to the other side while

23 he would send the crowds away. ·After sending
the crowds away he went up into the hills by
himself to pray. When evening came, he was
24 there alone, ·while the boat, by now far out on
the lake, was battling with a heavy sea, for there
25 was a head wind. ·In the fourth watch of the
night he went toward them, walking on the lake,
26 and when the disciples saw him walking on the
lake they were terrified. "It is a ghost," they said,
27 and cried out in fear. ·But at once Jesus called
out to them, saying, "Courage! It is I! Do not be
28 afraid." ·It was Peter who answered. "Lord," he
said, "if it is you, tell me to come to you across
29 the water." ·"Come," said Jesus. Then Peter
got out of the boat and started walking toward
30 Jesus across the water, ·but as soon as he felt the
force of the wind, he took fright and began to
31 sink. "Lord! Save me!" he cried. ·Jesus put out
his hand at once and held him. "Man of little
32 faith," he said, "why did you doubt?" ·And as
33 they got into the boat the wind dropped. ·The
men in the boat bowed down before him and
said, "Truly, you are the Son of God."
34 Having made the crossing, they came to land
35 at Gennesaret. ·When the local people recognized
him they spread the news through the whole
neighborhood and took all that were sick to him,
36 begging him just to let them touch the fringe of
his cloak. And all those who touched it were
completely cured.

✠

The opposition to Jesus cannot stifle his ministry.
Two great acts of power are now related. Jesus withdraws to a "lonely place," but the throngs pursue him
and are waiting on the shore. Matthew continues to
highlight Jesus as the compassionate healer who cannot
resist that tattered crowd (14). The first miracle of the

loaves (another will follow, in Chapter 15) demonstrates that compassion even further. The act of feeding the multitudes triggers a number of biblical images.
Moses was involved in feeding the people with manna
(Ex 16), and the great prophet Elisha multiplied food
for the hungry (2 K 4:42–44). Hopes for the Messianic kingdom were painted as a lavish feast with limitless food and drink (e.g. Is 25:6). Thus this miracle
story not only points to Jesus' compassion for the hunger of his people, but makes a strong biblical statement
about Jesus' identity.

Matthew's version of the story shows that the early
community continued to find new levels of symbolism
in this miracle. The ritual gestures of Jesus, the focus
on the bread (rather than the fish), and the careful
collection of the fragments have strong Eucharistic
overtones. And Matthew highlights the role of the disciples in the whole episode. They do not rudely oppose
Jesus (as they do in Mark 6:37) but are important
mediaries, who distribute the bread (14:19) and
gather the leftovers. The disciples share in Jesus' ministry.

The second miracle (22–33) is one of Matthew's
most effective passages. The basic details about Jesus'
miraculous walking on the water over an angry sea and
his mysterious encounter with the disciples and their
battered boat are all borrowed from Mark (6:45–52).
Both Gospels make a profound assertion about the divine power of Jesus, who like Yahweh himself treads
upon the crests of the sea (Jb 9:8) and whose majestic
words to the disciples, "Courage! It is I! Do not be
afraid," echo the revelatory words of the God of Israel
(cf. Is 41:4, 10; 43:25, etc.).

But Matthew enriches the story with material not

found in Mark. Peter, the consistent spokesman for the
disciples in this Gospel, asks to duplicate Jesus' own
dominance over the chaos of the sea (28). True to the
Gospel's assertion, the disciple *is* able to do the same
as Jesus (cf. 10:1). But, as he will do throughout the
Gospel, Matthew likes to pair the disciples' glory with
their flaws. Peter experiences the power of the chaos,
and fear begins to drag him down. His response is the
best instinctive response of the believer: "Lord, save
me!" Jesus instantly rescues Peter and, when all are in
the boat, the awed disciples worship Jesus with the
fullness of Christian faith: "Truly, you are the Son of
God" (33).

Mark's version of the story does not include the
Peter incident, and his portrait of the disciples presents
them as completely lacking in understanding or faith.
But, for Matthew, that boat crew images his own
church: buffeted, frightened, but clinging to belief,
"men of little faith" (cf. 6:30).

The chapter closes with the boat at shore and the
Gospel's repeated testimony to the healing power of
Jesus (14:36).

STUDY QUESTION: The Gospel stresses the inclusion of
the disciples in Jesus' power to feed
and to heal. Only fear stands in the
way of their ability to carry out
their mission. Does our own story
of Christian discipleship have any
parallels to the experiences of Peter
and the other disciples?

WHAT MAKES A MAN CLEAN?

¹
² **15** Pharisees and scribes from Jerusalem then came to Jesus and said. ·"Why do your disciples break away from the tradition of the elders? They do not wash their hands when they ³ eat food." ·"And why do you," he answered, "break away from the commandment of God for ⁴ the sake of your tradition? ·For God said: Do your duty to your father and mother and: Anyone who curses father or mother must be put to ⁵ death. ·But you say, 'If anyone says to his father or mother: Anything I have that I might have ⁶ used to help you is dedicated to God,' ·he is rid of his duty to father or mother. In this way you have made God's word null and void by ⁷ by means of your tradition. ·Hypocrites! It was you Isaiah meant when he so rightly prophesied:

⁸   This people honors me only with lip service, while their hearts are far from me.
⁹   The worship they offer me is worthless; the doctrines they teach are only human regulations."

¹⁰ He called the people to him and said, "Listen, ¹¹ and understand. ·What goes into the mouth does not make a man unclean; it is what comes out of the mouth that makes him unclean."

12   Then the disciples came to him and said, "Do
you know that the Pharisees were shocked when
13 they heard what you said?" ·He replied, "Any
plant my heavenly Father has not planted will be
14 pulled up by the roots. ·Leave them alone. They
are blind men leading blind men; and if one blind
man leads another, both will fall into a pit."

15   At this, Peter said to him, "Explain the parable
16 for us." ·Jesus replied, "Do even you not yet
17 understand? ·Can you not see that whatever goes
into the mouth passes through the stomach and is
18 discharged into the sewer? ·But the things that
come out of the mouth come from the heart, and
19 it is these that make a man unclean. ·For from the
heart come evil intentions: murder, adultery, for-
20 nication, theft, perjury, slander. ·These are the
things that make a man unclean. But to eat with
unwashed hands does not make a man unclean."

☩

The angry drone of Jesus' opponents returns, and
once again the issue is interpretation of the Law (cf.
12:1ff.; 5:17–48). Scribes and Pharisees "from Jerusalem" (the city where Jesus will meet his death) challenge Jesus because his disciples do not wash their
hands before eating, a practice not for purposes of hy-
giene but to prevent the ritual impurity caused by handling certain foods. The Temple priests were bound to
this by the Torah (Lv 22:4–7), but the obligation for
others was debated.

Jesus counters that the Pharisees' tradition can be at
odds with the very purpose of God's Law, as when
someone avoids supporting his parents by claiming that
the money had been vowed for Temple use. Many of
the rabbis had opposed this kind of abuse. For Jesus it

is a prime example of legalism gone sour. The searing quotation from Isaiah 29:13 indicts this wrongheaded perspective (8–9).

Jesus' teaching on the broader question of ritual purity is coupled with this dispute (10–20). It is likely that many of the early Christians continued to respect their Jewish heritage by abstaining from certain foods declared "unclean" by the Law and by rabbinic regulation. In Matthew's Gospel, Jesus stops short of nullifying this practice (note that Matthew omits Mark's verse "Thus he pronounced all foods clean"—7:19). But Jesus continues to be the great prophetic teacher who "fulfills" the Law by radically and unerringly pointing to its ultimate purpose. As Jesus' miniature parable states (11), it is not the food one eats that taints a person, but what comes out of the heart. The anger, the disrespect, the untruth that break the bond between people and reveal the twisted intentions of our heart—these are "impurity" worth our concern (19–20). Teachers in Israel (or anywhere else) concerned about less would feel the lash of Jesus' critique. They could pride themselves on being God's "vineyard" (cf. Is 5), but they would be jerked up by the roots. They may think the wisdom of the Law made them a light to the nations, but they have become sightless guides (12–14).

STUDY QUESTION: The Pharisees' concern for the peripheral and the nonessential is a caution for contemporary Christians. Jesus' challenge comes to us: what really makes a person "unclean"?

BREAD FOR THE OUTSIDERS

21 Jesus left that place and withdrew to the region
22 of Tyre and Sidon. ·Then out came a Canaanite
woman from that district and started shouting,
"Sir, Son of David, take pity on me. My daughter
23 is tormented by a devil." ·But he answered her not
a word. And his disciples went and pleaded with
him. "Give her what she wants," they said, "be-
24 cause she is shouting after us." ·He said in reply,
"I was sent only to the lost sheep of the House of
25 Israel." ·But the woman had come up and was
kneeling at his feet. "Lord," she said, "help me."
26 He replied, "It is not fair to take the children's
27 food and throw it to the house dogs." ·She retorted, "Ah yes, sir; but even house dogs can eat
the scraps that fall from their master's table."
28 Then Jesus answered her, "Woman, you have
great faith. Let your wish be granted." And from
that moment her daughter was well again.

29 Jesus went on from there and reached the
shores of the Sea of Galilee, and he went up into
30 the hills. He sat there, ·and large crowds came to
him bringing the lame, the crippled, the blind, the
dumb and many others; these they put down at
31 his feet, and he cured them. ·The crowds were
astonished to see the dumb speaking, the cripples
whole again, the lame walking and the blind with
their sight, and they praised the God of Israel.

32   But Jesus called his disciples to him and said,
"I feel sorry for all these people; they have been
with me for three days now and have nothing to
eat. I do not want to send them off hungry, they
33 might collapse on the way." ·The disciples said to
him. "Where could we get enough bread in this
34 deserted place to feed such a crowd?" ·Jesus said
to them. "How many loaves have you?" "Seven,"
35 they said, "and a few small fish." ·Then he in-
structed the crowd to sit down on the ground,
36 and he took the seven loaves and the fish, and he
gave thanks and broke them and handed them to
37 the disciples who gave them to the crowds. ·They
all ate as much as they wanted, and they collected
what was left of the scraps, seven baskets full.
38 Now four thousand men had eaten, to say nothing
39 of women and children. ·And when he had sent
the crowds away he got into the boat and went
to the district of Magadan.

✠

The argument with the scribes and Pharisees is broken off, and Jesus moves toward the northwestern bor-
der region of Tyre and Sidon. A gentile woman, a
Canaanite (Matthew may have pointedly labeled the
woman with the Old Testament's most common term
for the non-Israelite), startles the disciples by recognizing Jesus and asking a cure for her daughter. The
woman's faith—she calls Jesus "Lord" and "Son of
David," or Messiah—and Jesus' sharp reminder of his
mission to Israel (24) heightens the tension that the
Gospel story has been building. Jesus has respected the
destiny of the chosen people. He has come to restore
Israel. But their rejection of the gospel, and the open-
ness of gentiles such as this woman, signal a startling
development in God's plan of salvation. The "house

dogs" (a contemptuous term for gentiles) will eat the
bits of bread that fall from the table. The Gospel will
promise even more: the response of faith will become
the only entry to the Lord's banquet.

Jesus returns to Galilee ("Galilee of the nations," as
Matthew has named it—see 4:15). In terms hauntingly
similar to the great opening scene of Jesus' ministry
(4:23 to 5:1), the sick and the lame flow toward Israel's Messiah like a river of pain. He makes them
whole. These same people are miraculously fed
(32–39), a repeat of the multiplication of the loaves of
Chapter 14 (15–21).

Are these repetitions meant to foreshadow an eventual mission to the gentiles? Jesus himself will not go
beyond Israel. But after his death and resurrection, his
disciples will bring the nourishment of his graceful
words and his healing touch to all nations (see
28:16–20).

STUDY QUESTION: Matthew presents the tenacious faith
of the Canaanite woman as a pre-
view of the many "foreigners" who
would eventually seek healing and
nourishment in the message of
Jesus. How much does our faith
mean to us, who have become the
"children of the household"?

Matthew 16:1–12
BEWARE OF THE PHARISEE YEAST

¹ **16** The Pharisees and Sadducees came, and to
test him they asked if he would show them
² a sign from heaven. ·He replied, "In the evening
³ you say, 'It will be fine; there is a red sky,' ·and
in the morning, 'Stormy weather today; the sky
is red and overcast.' You know how to read the
face of the sky, but you cannot read the signs of
⁴ the times. ·It is an evil and unfaithful generation
that asks for a sign! The only sign it will be given
is the sign of Jonah." And leaving them standing
there, he went away.

⁵ The disciples, having crossed to the other shore,
⁶ had forgotten to take any food. ·Jesus said to
them, "Keep your eyes open, and be on your
guard against the yeast of the Pharisees and Sad-
⁷ ducees." ·And they said to themselves, "It is be-
⁸ cause we have not brought any bread." ·Jesus
knew it, and he said, "Men of little faith, why
are you talking among yourselves about having no
⁹ bread? ·Do you not yet understand? Do you not
remember the five loaves for the five thousand
¹⁰ and the number of baskets you collected? ·Or the
seven loaves for the four thousand and the num-
¹¹ ber of baskets you collected? ·How could you fail
to understand that I was not talking about bread?
What I said was: Beware of the yeast of the Phar-
¹² isees and Sadducees." ·Then they understood that

he was telling them to be on their guard, not
against the yeast for making bread, but against
the teaching of the Pharisees and Sadducees.

✠

Matthew continues to lace his account of Jesus' ministry with doses of opposition from the Jewish leaders.
The Pharisees, now joined by the Temple-based Sadducees, repeat their demands for a sign, but once again
their lack of faith is rebuffed (1–4). They will receive
no sign but the "sign of Jonah"; that is, Jesus' own
ministry and his death and resurrection (cf. 12:38–
42). The homespun verses about reading the "signs
of the times" (2–3) are probably later additions to
Matthew's text, since they are missing in most early
manuscripts.

Matthew's unique perception of the disciples stands
out in the brief discussion about "yeast" (5–12). In
Mark's version (see 8:14–21) the disciples' chronic
dullness and their abject inability to understand Jesus
reach a new low. They are perplexed at Jesus' warning
about the "yeast" of the Pharisees and Herodians
(Matthew changes this to the more familiar grouping,
Sadducees), and blink in confusion when he recalls the
great, Messianic miracle of the loaves. In Matthew the
disciples' image is more even-keeled. They have faith,
but only a "little," the designation consistently used by
the evangelist (16:8; 6:30). They understand, but
only gradually and with difficulty (12).

The sharp contrast between the disciples and the
Jewish leaders (evident since Chapter 11) helps pre-
pare for a major development in the Gospel story.
Peter's confession of Jesus as Messiah and Son of God

(16:16) will prompt Jesus to begin instructing his disciples on the meaning of his death and resurrection. But such contrast does not tempt Matthew to idealize the disciples. Even in Peter's moment of prominence he is evidently and painfully flawed.

STUDY QUESTION: The Gospel's portrayal of the disciples is honest and sympathetic: they are "of little faith." Can we recognize ourselves in the struggles and small triumphs of Jesus' followers?

PETER: FOUNDING ROCK

13 When Jesus came to the region of Caesarea
Philippi he put this question to his disciples, "Who
14 do people say the Son of Man is?" ·And they
said, "Some say he is John the Baptist, some
Elijah, and others Jeremiah or one of the proph-
15 ets." ·"But you," he said, "who do you say I am?"
16 Then Simon Peter spoke up. "You are the Christ,"
17 he said, "the Son of the living God." ·Jesus replied, "Simon son of Jonah, you are a happy
man! Because it was not flesh and blood that re-
18 vealed this to you but my Father in heaven. ·So
I now say to you: You are Peter and on this rock
I will build my Church. And the gates of the
19 underworld can never hold out against it. ·I will
give you the keys of the kingdom of heaven:
whatever you bind on earth shall be considered
bound in heaven; whatever you loose on earth
20 shall be considered loosed in heaven. ·Then he
gave the disciples strict orders not to tell anyone
that he was the Christ.

✠

In the northern Galilean city of Caesarea Philippi,
Jesus poses a fundamental question: "Who do people
say the Son of Man is?" (13). The disciples play back
the spectrum of popular opinion. When the question is

put directly to the disciples, it is Peter, their constant spokesman (cf. 15:15; 17:4, 24–27; 18:21; 19:27), who comes back with an unflinching confession of Jesus as "Christ" and "Son of the Living God" (16:16). Unlike Mark's Gospel, in which Jesus' identity remains veiled until the Passion, these titles come as no surprise in Matthew. Jesus has clearly been labeled as Messiah from his birth, and the disciples had proclaimed him Son of God after his appearance on the lake (cf. 14:33). This brace of titles is important here because they are proclaimed now *by Peter*. Such fidelity to Jesus is the foundation of the community's identity.

Confirmation of Peter's act of faith comes in words found only in Matthew (17–18). Peter is blessed because he has been gifted with understanding by the Father (cf. 11:25). And this Simon, "son of Jonah," will be known by a new name that reveals his role within the community. The material Matthew incorporates here may actually be playing on the identity of the Aramaic words for rock (*kepa*) and Peter (*kepa*). But beyond the wordplay an intriguing symbol is at work. Jewish reflection on the origin of the world had led to the belief that the foundation of the entire universe had been laid at Mount Zion, upon which stood the Temple. This was the centerpoint of the world. Is 28:16, a text that may have influenced Mt 16:17, speaks of this "rock": "See how I lay in Zion a stone of witness, a precious cornerstone, a foundation stone: The believer shall not stumble." The image of a world foundation stone which is also the foundation of the Temple points to the meaning of the "Peter" passage. On Peter, the leader of the disciples to whom will be entrusted Jesus' own ministry, a new "Temple" and a new community is being built: "On this rock I will build my *church*." Matthew is the only evangelist to use this technical term (see 18:17), which derives from the Hebrew word *qahal,* or "assembly," of the people of Israel. Against this foundation stone and the community built on it, even the forces of death will be powerless (18).

Peter's role as foundation rock brings with it new authority, and once again, the evangelist uses biblical and Jewish imagery to convey this. The disciple is given "the keys of the kingdom," a probable reference to Isaiah 22:22, where Eliakim is made prime minister of Judah in place of the faithless Shebna. Eliakim is given "the key of the House of David . . . ; should he open, no one shall close, should he close, no one shall open." And Peter, too, shall have such powers. He has the discretion of "binding" and "loosing," Jewish legal terms that referred either to the power of interpreting the obligations of the Law or to the power of excommunicating from the synagogue. It is not clear which of these is being conferred on Peter here (note that similar powers are given to the *community* in 18:18).

STUDY QUESTION: This passage is testimony to the continuity between Matthew's "church" and the life of Jesus. The community is distinctive because it follows Jesus and thus must share in the glory and the opposition that he himself experienced. Leadership in the community is validated if it is based on the kind of fidelity shown by Peter and the responsibility entrusted to him by Jesus.

"Destined to Go to Jerusalem"
The Fateful Pilgrimage from Galilee to Judea
Matthew 16:21 to 20:34

Matthew 16:21–28
DESTINY IN JERUSALEM

21   From that time Jesus began to make it clear to his disciples that he was destined to go to Jerusalem and suffer grievously at the hands of the elders and chief priests and scribes, to be put to
22 death and to be raised up on the third day. ·Then, taking him aside, Peter started to remonstrate with him. "Heaven preserve you, Lord"; he said,
23 "this must not happen to you." ·But he turned and said to Peter, "Get behind me, Satan! You are an obstacle in my path, because the way you think is not God's way but man's."
24   Then Jesus said to his disciples, "If anyone wants to be a follower of mine, let him renounce
25 himself and take up his cross and follow me. ·For anyone who wants to save his life will lose it; but anyone who loses his life for my sake will find it.
26 What, then, will a man gain if he wins the whole world and ruins his life? Or what has a man to offer in exchange for his life?
27   "For the Son of Man is going to come in the glory of his Father with his angels, and, when he does, he will reward each one according to his
28 behavior. ·I tell you solemnly, there are some of these standing here who will not taste death before they see the Son of Man coming with his kingdom."

✠

Peter's confession and his designation as leader of a new, elect community preface a major turn in the Gospel story. "From that time"—the same deliberate phrase that marked the beginning of Jesus' ministry in Galilee (cf. 4:17)—signals a new phase of that ministry as Jesus openly speaks of his death in Jerusalem (21). This is the first of four such predictions in Matthew's Gospel (cf. 17:22–23; 20:17–19; 26:1–2), which project a sense of inevitable death yet certain vindication. This mood of vindication is implied in the time phrase taken from Hosea 6:3, a text that confidently asserts that "on the third day" Yahweh will "raise up" his beloved. A Jesus without the Passion is simply incomprehensible from the Gospel's perspective. His selfless giving of life and the validation of that gift in resurrection are the clearest statements of his mission (20:28).

That is why Peter's resistance to the idea of Jesus' suffering is taken so seriously by the gospel writers. In Matthew's account the shock of Peter's obtuseness is deepened. The apostle is not only called "Satan," the tempter who seeks to subvert Jesus' purpose (as the prince of evil did in Chapter 4), but he is also an "obstacle" or literally a "stumbling block" in Jesus' way. Matthew continues his calculated mix of the disciple's image. Peter, the "founding rock" on which the community is built, is also capable of being a "stumbling block" who stands in the way by making judgments from the wrong perspective (cf. this alternate image of "rock" in Isaiah 8:14).

The right perspective, Jesus' own, is reiterated by a

series of sayings calling for selfless dedication to the Gospel (24–26). Following Jesus has its cost: one must go to Jerusalem. But such fidelity also has its reward. The "Son of Man," a title for Jesus used in contexts both of suffering and of judgment, will come to reward each one "according to his behavior" (27), a constant refrain in Matthew. The saying in verse 28 may originally have referred to an immediate expectation of the Son's glorious return. But now within the context of Matthew's Gospel it probably refers to the triumphant appearance of the risen Jesus which concludes the Gospel (cf. 28:16–20).

STUDY QUESTION: Many of us might be tempted, as Peter was, to think of Christianity without the cross. But "giving of life" is at the heart of the Gospel and cannot be shunted aside.

Matthew 17:1–20
JESUS—SON AND LORD:
THE VISION OF TRANSFIGURATION

¹ 17 Six days later, Jesus took with him Peter and James and his brother John and led them up a high mountain where they could be ² alone. ·There in their presence he was transfigured: his face shone like the sun and his clothes ³ became as white as the light. ·Suddenly Moses and Elijah appeared to them; they were talking ⁴ with him. ·Then Peter spoke to Jesus. "Lord," he said, "it is wonderful for us to be here; if you wish, I will make three tents here, one for you, ⁵ one for Moses and one for Elijah." ·He was still speaking when suddenly a bright cloud covered them with shadow, and from the cloud there came a voice which said, "This is my Son, the Be- ⁶ loved; he enjoys my favor. Listen to him." ·When they heard this, the disciples fell on their faces, ⁷ overcome with fear. ·But Jesus came up and touched them. "Stand up," he said, "do not be ⁸ afraid." ·And when they raised their eyes they saw no one but only Jesus.

⁹ As they came down from the mountain Jesus gave them this order, "Tell no one about the vision until the Son of Man has risen from the ¹⁰ dead." ·And the disciples put this question to him, "Why do the scribes say then that Elijah has ¹¹ to come first?" ·"True," he replied, "Elijah is to

come to see that everything is once more as it
12 should be; ·however, I tell you that Elijah has
come already and they did not recognize him but
treated him as they pleased; and the Son of Man
13 will suffer similarly at their hands." ·The disciples
understood then that he had been speaking of
John the Baptist.
14   As they were rejoining the crowd a man came
up to him and went down on his knees before
15 him. ·"Lord," he said, "take pity on my son: he
is a lunatic and in a wretched state; he is always
16 falling into the fire or into the water. ·I took him
to your disciples and they were unable to cure
17 him." ·"Faithless and perverse generation!" Jesus
said in reply. "How much longer must I be with
you? How much longer must I put up with you?
18 Bring him here to me." ·And when Jesus rebuked
it the devil came out of the boy who was cured
from that moment.
19   Then the disciples came privately to Jesus.
"Why were we unable to cast it out?" they asked.
20 He answered, "Because you have little faith. I tell
you solemnly, if your faith were the size of a
mustard seed you could say to this mountain,
'Move from here to there,' and it would move;
nothing would be impossible for you."

✠

"Six days later. . . ." The words bind the haunting
vision of the transfiguration to the preceding event of
Peter's confession and Jesus' prediction of his fate in
Jerusalem. Each of these episodes concentrates on the
identity of Jesus and its implication for the disciples.

Matthew lingers over this scene's majestic portrait of
Jesus. A number of details evoke the story of Sinai and
seem to subtly reinforce the image of Jesus as the "new
Moses": The incident takes place on a "mountain";

Jesus' transfigured face shines "like the sun" (cf. Ex 34:29, 35); he converses with "Moses and Elijah" (symbolic of the "Law and the Prophets," Matthew's typical way of speaking of the Scriptures); a "bright cloud," a sign of the Lord's presence at Sinai and in the desert, overshadows them (cf. Ex 24:15–18).

Not only is Jesus the new Moses, the true lawgiver, but he is the "Son." Matthew repeats word for word the Father's declaration at the baptism (5). Jesus is the truly obedient Israelite who enjoys a unique relationship to the Father. He is the one who reveals the will of his Father to those he chooses (cf. 11:27). Thus the believer must hear this voice: "listen to him." Jesus has already been to the "mountain" in Matthew's Gospel (cf. 5:1) and, brimming with authority, had brought the Mosaic Law to its fulfillment. At the conclusion of the Gospel, the risen Lord will stand once again on a mountain, and his authoritative word will plunge his disciples into a new mission (28:16–20). But before that time comes, Jesus must experience suffering and death. As this dark chapter of the Gospel begins to unfold, the transfiguration scene reminds us of Jesus' true identity.

Matthew also gives careful attention to the reaction of the disciples. In Mark, the transfiguration becomes an occasion for further display of the disciples' ineptness. Peter is incoherent (9:6), and the rest gape in uncomprehending fear (9:6, 8, 10). Not so in Matthew. The reaction of the disciples corresponds to the majesty of Jesus. Peter addresses his transfigured master as "Lord," and his offer to set up commemorative booths is properly deferential ("if you wish"). At the sound of the voice from heaven, the disciples are gripped with reverential fear and prostrate in adoration (6). The account ends with an exquisite detail found only in Matthew (7). Jesus comes forward and soothes their terror with a healing touch: "Stand up, do not be afraid." In Jesus, divine majesty and gentle compassion meet.

As Jesus and his disciples descend the mountain, the gloom of opposition and impending death appears (9–13). Matthew uses the conversation about Elijah to return to a consideration of John, whose fate is a forecast of Jesus' own. John is that "Elijah" who was expected to herald the coming of the kingdom. But before the arrival of this glorious moment, both John and Jesus will experience rejection and death (12).

The disciples have been able to absorb this warning of Jesus (13), but their faith remains weak. Their "little faith" (20) once again prevents them from carrying out the mission of life entrusted to them. Earlier, Peter had allowed fear and "little faith" to stifle his power over the chaos of the sea (14:30). The same things happen again. The "little faith" of the disciples has stopped them from curing a young man seized with the spirit of lunacy. But if a disciple allows the power of God to work through him, "nothing would be impossible."

STUDY QUESTION: The transfiguration confronts us with the full mystery of Christ: Jesus en route to his death, but the glory of his triumphant resurrection already putting that death into new perspective. Christian faith enables us to put our own experience of suffering and death in the perspective of Christ's resurrection.

Matthew 17:22–27
DEATH AND TAXES

22 One day when they were together in Galilee,
Jesus said to them, "The Son of Man is going to
23 be handed over into the power of men; ·they will
put him to death, and on the third day he will be
raised to life again." And a great sadness came
over them.
24 When they reached Capernaum, the collectors
of the half shekel came to Peter and said, "Does
25 your master not pay the half shekel?" ·"Oh yes,"
he replied, and went into the house. But before he
could speak, Jesus said, "Simon, what is your
opinion? From whom do the kings of the earth
take toll or tribute? From their sons or from for-
26 eigners?" ·And when he replied, "From foreigners," Jesus said, "Well then, the sons are exempt.
27 However, so as not to offend these people, go to
the lake and cast a hook; take the first fish that
bites, open its mouth and there you will find a
shekel; take it and give it to them for me and for
you."

✠

In the following chapter we will come to the fourth
of Matthew's major discourses (18:1–35), another
composite of Jesus' sayings and parables dealing with

the kind of relationship that should bind together those who belong to the kingdom of God. These few verses serve as a remote preparation for the discourse.

Jesus gathers his disciples together like a commander rallying his troops before a battle. A second time, he predicts the death and victory that awaits him in Jerusalem. Matthew's portrayal of the disciples continues to be distinctively different from Mark's. Matthew observes that the disciples are saddened by the prediction of death; in Mark we are told: ". . . they did not understand what he said and were afraid to ask him" (9:32).

The band now moves to the seaside town of Capernaum, where an incident recorded only by Matthew takes place (24–27). Tax collectors approach Peter (confirming his leadership role, blessed in 16:17–19) and ask if Jesus pays the "half-shekel" tax. Prior to A.D. 70, this tax was levied by the Jews for the upkeep of the Temple (cf. Ex 30:13). To pay it was a sign of solidarity with the Jewish people. Peter insists that his master does pay the tax, but once he is inside the house, Jesus uses the question as a teaching moment. Jesus and his followers are not "foreigners" but "sons" of the King. Therefore they are free from the obligation of any such tribute.

The story concludes with the decision to pay the tax "so as not to offend these people" (27). In a rather spectacular way, God's providence assures Peter the means of paying. This story was undoubtedly instruction for Matthew's church. Even though Christians were free, they might still observe some laws and customs out of consideration for Jewish sensibilities. Within the flow of the Gospel, this story has another function. The disciples are "sons" of the King; what determines true greatness within this kingdom? That is the question that leads into the discourse of Chapter 18.

STUDY QUESTION: The gospel tradition, like Paul, proclaims that to be a Christian is to be truly free. But freedom must always be exercised with respect for the conscience of the less free. Such compassionate sensitivity is a hallmark of those who belong to the kingdom.

Matthew 18:1–35
DISCOURSE ON LIFE IN THE COMMUNITY OF JESUS

The fourth great discourse of the Gospel lifts up the essential qualities that should characterize those who belong to the community of Jesus.

The discourse, a composite of parables and sayings, can be divided into two main sections. The first half (1–14) deals with the church's responsibility to the "little ones," an affectionate term for the weak and straying members of the community. The second section (15–35) reflects on the ties that bind the "brethren" together. Each section is molded by a similar pattern: a series of sayings is followed by a parable and sealed by a reference to the will of the Father in heaven (see 18:14, 35). Thus two characteristic concerns of Matthew's Gospel are joined: the responsibilities of discipleship and the search for God's will. The whole is directed to the "disciples," and it is obvious that through these followers of Jesus the evangelist intends to strike home to the leaders and people of his own church.

Matthew 18:1–14
CONCERN FOR THE "LITTLE ONES"

¹ 18 At this time the disciples came to Jesus and said, "Who is the greatest in the kingdom ² of heaven?" ·So he called a little child to him and ³ set the child in front of them. ·Then he said, "I tell you solemnly, unless you change and become like little children you will never enter the king- ⁴ dom of heaven. ·And so, the one who makes him- self as little as this little child is the greatest in the kingdom of heaven.

⁵ "Anyone who welcomes a little child like this ⁶ in my name welcomes me. ·But anyone who is an obstacle to bring down one of these little ones who have faith in me would be better drowned in the depths of the sea with a great millstone ⁷ around his neck. ·Alas for the world that there should be such obstacles! Obstacles indeed there must be, but alas for the man who provides them!

⁸ "If your hand or your foot should cause you to sin, cut it off and throw it away: it is better for you to enter into life crippled or lame, than to have two hands or two feet and be thrown into ⁹ eternal fire. ·And if your eye should cause you to sin, tear it out and throw it away: it is better for you to enter into life with one eye, than to have two eyes and be thrown into the hell of fire.

¹⁰ "See that you never despise any of these little ones, for I tell you that their angels in heaven

are continually in the presence of my Father in heaven.

12 "Tell me. Suppose a man has a hundred sheep and one of them strays; will he not leave the ninety-nine on the hillisde and go in search of
13 the stray? ·I tell you solemnly, if he finds it, it gives him more joy than do the ninety-nine that
14 did not stray at all. ·Similarly, it is never the will of your Father in heaven that one of these little ones should be lost.

✠

The discourse opens with the thematic question of the disciples: "Who is the greatest in the kingdom of heaven?" Jesus jolts the disciples by placing a child before them. To even enter the kingdom (let alone find rank within it) one must undergo a complete conversion (literally "turn" around) and become "like little children" (3). The image of becoming a child is not an appeal for a romantic naïveté but a demand for genuine humility. The Christian must sense an utter dependence upon God for life and for every gift. Humility and lack of self-concern are appealing instincts in a child but hard-earned virtues for an adult. Jesus cites them as the fruits of genuine conversion and true greatness.

The image of a child begins to shift in verse 5. It now becomes a designation for a member of the community. Jesus identifies with a "child like this" and, as the mission discourse had already proclaimed (10:40), to show hospitality to such a Christian is to receive the Lord, who is always with them. Suddenly, in verse 6, the image of a "child" slides into that of "little ones." The same sense of humility and lack of pretense covers both terms, but "little ones" refers to the Christian not as a fresh example of a converted life but as a member of a community who is weak and faltering in faith.

To be an "obstacle" to them (a good literal rendition of the Greek term *skandalon*, which is used throughout this section) is a terrible crime against someone who, though weak, believes in Jesus (6). The English word "scandal" can be restricted to doing something so enticingly evil that others are drawn into the sin (as the translation of the word *skandalizein* as "cause to sin" in verses 8 and 9 implies). But the Greek word *skandalon* means a "stumbling block" (cf. 16:23) and thus could refer to a whole spectrum of obstacles thrown in the way of a weak person. It might be the allure of sin that pushes them further away, or it might be the incompassionate glare of the righteous that blocks their return. To be such an obstacle is a mortal break in the sensitive and compassionate response that the members of the community owe each other (5–7). To avoid being such an obstacle calls for dramatic, decisive action (8–9).

As Matthew continues to emphasize, the Father's unceasing love for his people is the ultimate source and model of Jesus' own compassion and of the mandate he gives his disciples (cf. 5:43–48). This dimension is introduced in verse 10. These "little ones" have their own angels before the Father in heaven. The Judaism of Jesus' and Matthew's day had become increasingly intrigued by angels, and some Jewish literature had spoken of individual protecting angels. But to speak of these angels as having constant access to Yahweh is unique and makes an eloquent testimony to the Father's particular concern for the weak.

That concern is amplified in Matthew's version of

the parable of the lost sheep (12–14). In Luke's Gospel the same parable (15:3–7) stresses the Father's joy over the repentance of one sinner, and is used by Jesus as a justification for his own ministry of forgiveness to the outcasts. Matthew shifts the focus of the parable by linking it to the theme of responsibility to the weak. The Gospel has already documented Jesus' own pastoral concern for "lost" and "confused" sheep (see 9:36; 10:6; 15:24). Now the disciples must accept this responsibility as their own. The refrain of the Father's will concludes this major section. Not one of these little ones should be lost. Since this is the Father's will, it must become an urgent priority of the community.

STUDY QUESTION: This section of the discourse emphasizes that a relentless compassion for the weak and the outcasts must be a central characteristic of the Christian community. How does our church or parish measure up to this gospel demand?

Matthew 18:15–35
FORGIVENESS FOR THE BRETHREN

15 "If your brother does something wrong, go and have it out with him alone, between your two selves. If he listens to you, you have won back
16 your brother. ·If he does not listen, take one or two others along with you: the evidence of two or three witnesses is required to sustain any charge.
17 But if he refuses to listen to these, report it to the community; and if he refuses to listen to the community, treat him like a pagan or a tax collector.

18 "I tell you solemnly, whatever you bind on earth shall be considered bound in heaven: whatever you loose on earth shall be considered loosed in heaven.

19 "I tell you solemnly once again, if two of you on earth agree to ask anything at all, it will be
20 granted to you by my Father in heaven. ·For where two or three meet in my name, I shall be there with them."

21 Then Peter went up to him and said, "Lord, how often must I forgive my brother if he wrongs
22 me? As often as seven times?" ·Jesus answered, "Not seven, I tell you, but seventy-seven times.

23 "And so the kingdom of heaven may be compared to a king who decided to settle his accounts
24 with his servants. ·When the reckoning began, they brought him a man who owed ten thou-
25 sand talents; ·but he had no means of paying, so his master gave orders that he should be sold,

together with his wife and children and all his
26 possessions, to meet the debt. •At this, the servant
threw himself down at his master's feet. 'Give me
time,' he said, 'and I will pay the whole sum.'
27 And the servant's master felt so sorry for him
28 that he let him go and canceled the debt. •Now as
this servant went out, he happened to meet a fellow servant who owed him one hundred denarii;
and he seized him by the throat and began to
29 throttle him. 'Pay what you owe me,' he said. •His
fellow servant fell at his feet and implored him,
30 saying, 'Give me time and I will pay you.' •But
the other would not agree; on the contrary, he
had him thrown into prison till he should pay the
31 debt. •His fellow servants were deeply distressed
when they saw what had happened, and they
went to their master and reported the whole affair
32 to him. •Then the master sent for him. "You
wicked servant,' he said, 'I canceled all that debt
33 of yours when you appealed to me. •Were you
not bound, then, to have pity on your fellow ser-
34 vant just as I had pity on you?' •And in his anger
the master handed him over to the torturers till
35 he should pay all his debt. •And that is how my
heavenly Father will deal with you unless you
each forgive your brother from your heart."

✠

The priority of compassion in the community does
not mean permissiveness. The second half of the discourse opens with the outline of a procedure for
dealing with a recalcitrant "brother" (15–18). Sensitivity demands that the fault be dealt with discreetly.
But if that fails, help should be sought from others
(following the injunction of Deuteronomy 19:15,
which called for two or three witnesses in major court
proceedings). If even this step is rebuffed, then the

brother is to be brought before the entire community (Matthew uses the technical term "church," as in 16:18. Here it probably refers to a local church). The community is invested with the power of binding and loosing (18, cf. 16:19), which apparently refers to the authority of excommunication. The erring brother is to be considered as a "tax collector" or a "pagan," that is, as an outsider in need of conversion. The use of these labels for the "outsider" might also subtly remind the community of the fact that Jesus had particular compassion for such as these (cf. 11:19).

This method is not unlike procedures used in some Jewish communities (such as the reform group at Qumran). Matthew's own church may have adopted similar methods for handling members whose behavior was seriously incompatible with the demands of the gospel. But the setting in which this procedure is placed indicates that the priority of compassion is not forgotten. First of all, it is followed by a solemn saying of Jesus on the power of united prayer (19). Presumably, one of the objects of such prayer would be to "win back" a brother where all other efforts seem futile. The cohesive center of this praying community is ultimately the presence of Jesus. A Jewish saying promised that wherever two people discussed the Law, the *Shekinah* (or divine presence) was with them. As Matthew has done before (cf. 11:28–30), sayings dealing with the Law are transferred to Jesus. Fidelity to the words of Jesus ("God-with-us") brings his sustaining presence into the midst of the believers (cf. 1:23; 28:30).

Divisive wrongdoing calls for prudent action and sensitive correction. But even if radical discipline is necessary, compassion and forgiveness remain the only stance possible among members of the community.

Peter's question (21) swings the chapter fully back to this dominant theme. His words probe the limits of forgiveness. Jesus' reply appears to reverse the words of Lamech in Genesis (4:24), in which this descendant of Cain called for blood vengeance seventy times seven. Now this becomes a number symbolic of limitless forgiveness.

The parable that concludes the chapter (23–35) is found only in Matthew and is typical of the scarcely veiled allegory that characterizes his style. The story of the king and his servant illustrates why forgiveness is so necessary. The servant owes a staggering debt to the king (ten thousand talents is an astronomical figure in first-century economics) but is forgiven out of pity and the debt completely canceled (27). But this forgiven servant soon forgets his own situation and treats viciously a fellow servant who owes him a minor sum. The other servants can only be depressed at such blind behavior (31), and the king is provoked to anger. Matthew's favorite theme, responsibility and judgment, is played out again when the unforgiving servant is made to pay for his behavior (34–35).

The closing verse echoes Matthew's stress in the Lord's Prayer and the Sermon on the Mount (cf. 6:12, 14–15; 5:43–48). If we do not forgive "from the heart," then we simply do not recognize our own status as "forgiven servants" and we certainly do not know the Father revealed by Jesus.

STUDY QUESTION: Why does Matthew's Gospel make forgiveness such a pressing concern for the followers of Jesus? The answer to that question reveals the heart of the Gospel.

Matthew 19:1–15
NEW TEACHING IN JUDEA: DIVORCE

¹ 19 Jesus had now finished what he wanted to say, and he left Galilee and came into the part of Judea which is on the far side of the Jordan. ² ·Large crowds followed him and he healed them there.

³ Some Pharisees approached him, and to test him they said, "Is it against the Law for a man ⁴ to divorce his wife on any pretext whatever?" ·He answered, "Have you not read that the creator from the beginning made them male and female ⁵ and then he said: This is why a man must leave father and mother, and cling to his wife, and the ⁶ two become one body? ·They are no longer two, therefore, but one body. So then, what God has united, man must not divide."

⁷ They said to him, "Then why did Moses command that a writ of dismissal should be given in ⁸ case of divorce?" ·"It was because you were so unteachable," he said, "that Moses allowed you to divorce your wives, but it was not like this from ⁹ the beginning. ·Now I say this to you: the man who divorces his wife—I am not speaking of fornication—and marries another, is guilty of adultery."

¹⁰ The disciples said to him, "If that is how things are between husband and wife, it is not advisable ¹¹ to marry." ·But he replied, "It is not everyone

who can accept what I have said, but only those
12 to whom it is granted. ·There are eunuchs born
that way from their mother's womb, there are
eunuchs made so by men and there are eunuchs
who have made themselves that way for the sake
of the kingdom of heaven. Let anyone accept this
who can."
13 People brought little children to him, for him to
lay his hands on them and say a prayer. The dis-
14 ciples turned them away, ·but Jesus said, "Let the
little children alone, and do not stop them coming
to me; for it is to such as these that the kingdom
15 of heaven belongs." ·Then he laid his hands on
them and went on his way.

☩

Matthew's standard transitional formula (cf. 7:28)
signals another milestone in the Gospel story. With the
discourse on community life now finished, Jesus moves
from Galilee into Judea. According to Matthew's account, this is the first time Jesus has returned to the
southern region since he and his parents escaped the
tentacles of Herod (cf. 2:14, 22). Now Jesus is back,
followed by large crowds and brandishing his healing
power (2). Judea and its capital city, Jerusalem, will
have another chance to lash out at this one "born king
of the Jews (2:2).

As Jesus moves into Judean territory, he is confronted by some Pharisees, who try to snare him with a
question about the Law (3-4): Is it against the Law to
divorce one's wife "on any pretext whatever?" The
question seems to reflect a first-century debate between
two rabbinic schools on how to interpret Deuteronomy
24:1. The school of Shammai taught that divorce was
permitted only on the grounds of adultery, while the

school of Hillel allowed divorce "on any pretext whatever."

In Matthew's version of this story, Jesus refuses to accept the debate on these terms and immediately appeals to a text of the Law he considers most fundamental, and therefore binding, in this question. Jesus cites Genesis 1:27 and 2:24 to illustrate that the will of the "creator" is that husband and wife enjoy intimate and unbreakable union (4–6). In typical rabbinic style, the Pharisees counter with the text of Deuteronomy 24:1, which assumes that divorce is permissible. But Jesus will not allow this as a decisive text. Moses permitted divorce only as a concession to the moral immaturity of the people.

In a solemn manner (9), Jesus concludes the debate with his own authoritative interpretation of the Law. "The man who divorces his wife . . . and marries another, is guilty of adultery." Imbedded in this statement is an apparent qualification that continues to baffle interpreters. Literally the phrase says, "except for uncleanness" (*porneia*, a general term in Greek). The Jerusalem Bible translation—"I am not speaking of fornication"—reflects one solution that considers the whole question of *porneia* (translated as "fornication") as put to one side. But it seems preferable both here and in the other Matthaean text, of 5:32, to translate the Greek in its usual sense of "except," that is, as some sort of qualification introduced into Jesus' originally unqualified prohibition (cf. Mk 10:11–12; Lk 16:18).

Two solutions seem most possible. One is to translate *porneia* as "adultery." Thus the saying of Jesus would prohibit divorce "except in the case of adultery." Matthew's Jewish-Christian community may have adapted the prohibition to their own circumstances. The weakness of this "solution" is that it makes Jesus' statement in verse 9 anticlimactic. He ends up accepting one side of a rabbinic debate that he initially had radically challenged! For this reason, some commentators prefer to understand *porneia* as referring to marriages that violated the strict Jewish laws of consanguinity (the word *porneia* is used this way in Acts 15:29). In this case, the adapted saying of Jesus would be directed to gentiles who, prior to their conversion, were married to women within the restricted line of blood relationship. Before being accepted into the community, they would have to sever this illicit marriage bond; hence, Jesus' prohibition against divorce allows this kind of "exception."

No solution can be definitive, because there is no way of knowing exactly what the "exceptive clause" meant to Matthew's readers. But whatever the solution might be, it must be compatible with the demand for "deeper" holiness (see 5:20) that underlies so much of Jesus' teaching during this measured journey to Jerusalem. The reaction of the disciples (10–12) confirms this. Jesus' demand for indissoluble unity in marriage and his prohibition of remarriage seem like impossible ideals. His reply offers no concession. The ability to respond to the gospel is a gift (11), but a gift that can move the disciple to a genuine holiness. He uses a startling image. Eunuchs were despised in Jewish society; Deuteronomy 23:1 forbade their participation in the assembly of Yahweh, although later rabbinic interpretation of that text permitted eunuchs entry. In Jesus' view there can be those who renounce the use of sex not because of impotence or accident but "for the sake of the kingdom of heaven." This may refer to both those who are unable to remarry (cf. 19:9) and celibates who forgo marriage to free themselves for the gospel mission.

As if to restate the need for radical response to the Gospel, the section concluded with the image of the child. People were bringing their children to Jesus to be blessed, and he uses the moment to remind his disciples that the kingdom belongs to those who, like children, acknowledge their needs without pretense (cf. 18:2f.).

STUDY QUESTION: Each of the synoptic Gospels testifies to Jesus' teaching on the indissolubility of marriage. What does this say about the meaning of marriage and the ideal of love and union the Gospel presumes between married Christians?

Matthew 19:16 to 20:16
THE DEMANDS AND REWARDS
OF DISCIPLESHIP

16 And there was a man who came to him and asked, "Master, what good deed must I do to
17 possess eternal life?" ·Jesus said to him, "Why do you ask me about what is good? There is one alone who is good. But if you wish to enter into
18 life, keep the commandments." ·He said, "Which." "These": Jesus replied, "You must not kill. You must not commit adultery. You must not steal.
19 You must not bring false witness. ·Honor your father and mother, and: you must love your
20 neighbor as yourself." ·The young man said to him, "I have kept all these. What more do I need
21 to do?" ·Jesus said, "If you wish to be perfect, go and sell what you own and give the money to the poor, and you will have treasure in heaven; then
22 come, follow me." ·But when the young man heard these words he went away sad, for he was a man of great wealth.
23 Then Jesus said to his disciples, "I tell you solemnly, it will be hard for a rich man to enter the
24 kingdom of heaven. ·Yes, I tell you again, it is easier for a camel to pass through the eye of a needle than for a rich man to enter the kingdom
25 of heaven." ·When the disciples heard this they were astonished. "Who can be saved, then?" they

26 said. ·Jesus gazed at them. "For men," he told them, "this is impossible; for God everything is possible."

27 Then Peter spoke. "What about us?" he said to him. "We have left everything and followed you.

28 What are we to have, then?" ·Jesus said to him, "I tell you solemnly, when all is made new and the Son of Man sits on his throne of glory, you will yourselves sit on twelve thrones to judge the

29 twelve tribes of Israel. ·And everyone who has left houses, brothers, sisters, father, mother, children or land for the sake of my name will be repaid a hundred times over, and also inherit eternal life.

30 "Many who are first will be last, and the last, first.

1 20 "Now the kingdom of heaven is like a landowner going out at daybreak to hire

2 workers for his vineyard. ·He made an agreement with the workers for one denarius a day, and sent

3 them to his vineyard. ·Going out at about the third hour he saw others standing idle in the mar-

4 ket place ·and said to them, 'You go to my vine-

5 yard too and I will give you a fair wage.' ·So they went. At about the sixth hour and again at about the ninth hour, he went out and did the

6 same. ·Then at about the eleventh hour he went out and found more men standing around, and he said to them, 'why have you been standing here

7 idle all day?' ·'Because no one has hired us,' they answered. He said to them, 'You go into my vine-

8 yard too,' ·In the evening, the owner of the vineyard said to his bailiff, 'Call the workers and pay them their wages, starting with the last arrivals

9 and ending with the first.' ·So those who were hired at about the eleventh hour came forward

10 and received one denarius each. ·When the first came, they expected to get more, but they too re-

11 ceived one denarius each. ·They took it, but

12 grumbled at the landowner. ·'The men who came last,' they said, 'have done only one hour, and you have treated them the same as us, though we have
13 done a heavy day's work in all the heat.' ·He answered one of them and said, 'My friend, I am not being unjust to you; did we not agree on one
14 denarius? ·Take your earnings and go. I choose to pay the last comer as much as I pay you.
15 Have I no right to do what I like with my own?
16 Why be envious because I am generous?' ·Thus the last will be first, and the first, last."

✠

This section continues the Gospel's concern with the cost of discipleship, a theme that has permeated Jesus' teaching on the road to Jerusalem.

A man approaches Jesus (16–22) and asks a question that has dominated Matthew's Gospel: "Master, what good deed must I do to possess eternal life?" It is not a question about frills; it is basic and practical. And it recognizes Jesus as the Teacher, capable of giving an answer. Jesus takes this question at face value: ". . . if you wish to enter into life," keep the Law, in which God's will has been made clear. Jesus ticks off the commands that deal with relationships, climaxing in the love command (as he did in 5:43–48). But the young man, again in tune with Matthew's Gospel, senses that Jesus' teaching calls for something more (20). To be "perfect," the young man must put aside his wealth and "follow" Jesus.

"Perfect": the Greek word is exactly that used in 5:48, where Jesus capped his teaching on the fulfillment of the Law. To be so animated by love that one can love an enemy—this is to be "complete" or "perfect" as the heavenly Father is perfect.

In the Sermon on the Mount Jesus had defined "perfect" through his teaching on the love command. Here, in Chapter 19, "perfection" is defined as putting aside everything in order to "follow" Jesus. The two definitions are the same, because Jesus carries out his own commands. To "follow him" is to fulfill the Law of love. The invitations offered to the young man—"if you wish to enter into life," "if you wish to be perfect. . . ," and "come, follow me"—make it clear that this passage is not an instruction for an elite, but the basic gospel call for *all* those who would follow Jesus. Every obstacle to genuine discipleship must be put aside. For the young man, the cost is too high, and he turns away with regret (19:22).

Jesus' teaching on marriage had staggered the disciples (19:10). His blunt words on the obstacle that wealth throws in the way of discipleship are no more digestible (23–26). Matthew does not present Jesus as an ideologue who opposes wealth on the basis of a particular social theory. Jesus is pragmatic: much wealth tends to demand total allegiance. So does God's kingdom. Jesus had already drawn the common-sense conclusion: "You cannot be the slave both of God and of money" (6:24). Therefore a rich man is as likely to shed the encumbrances of wealth as a camel is to slip through the eye of a needle! Jesus' impossible hyperbole should not be diluted (the needle's eye was not a gate in the wall of Jerusalem at the time of Jesus, as some commentators have suggested).

The disciples' distraught question catches Jesus' point (25) and enables him to restore their perspective: the ability to respond to the gospel is never earned, by either rich or poor. It is a gift (26). The Twelve were given that gift, and Peter, their spokesman, asks about the consequences. They are promised a place of authority at the moment of judgment (28). They are the foundations of the new Israel Jesus has come to build. They and all who put aside any obstacle to following Jesus will inherit what the rich young man found too costly: "eternal life" (29).

Discipleship as an interplay of gift, and response is the focus of the thoughtful parable that concludes this section (20:1-15). Matthew frames it with two enigmatic proverbs that hint at presumption deflated, at expectation reversed: the first last, the last first (19:30; 20:16). And that, in fact, is the message of the parable. The King is like a vineyard owner who hires from a labor pool at various hours of the day. When evening comes, everyone, even those hired at the last hour, are paid the same. Those first called protest such injustice. But the parable cleverly spears the listener on his own indignation. It is not a commentary on social justice but on the unexpected generosity of God, who gifts whom he will and when he will. Discipleship is never earned, only given. All that is asked of the one called is response, however and whenever the call comes.

STUDY QUESTION: The story of the rich young man invites us to search our own lives for the obstacles that stand in the way of following Jesus. The disciples' question and the parable of the vineyard laborers remind us that only God's power can truly free us enough to be a disciple.

Matthew 20:17–34
UP TO JERUSALEM

17 Jesus was going up to Jerusalem, and on the way he took the Twelve to one side and said to
18 them, ·"Now we are going up to Jerusalem, and the Son of Man is about to be handed over to the chief priests and scribes. They will condemn
19 him to death ·and will hand him over to the pagans to be mocked and scourged and crucified; and on the third day he will rise again."
20 Then the mother of Zebedee's sons came with her sons to make a request of him, and bowed
21 low; ·and he said to her, "What is it you want?" She said to him, "Promise that these two sons of mine may sit one at your right hand and the
22 other at your left in your kingdom." ·"You do not know what you are asking," Jesus answered. "Can you drink the cup that I am going to
23 drink?" They replied, "We can." ·"Very well," he said, "you shall drink my cup, but as for seats at my right hand and my left, these are not mine to grant; they belong to those to whom they have been allotted by my Father."
24 When the other ten heard this they were indig-
25 nant with the two brothers. ·But Jesus called them to him and said, "You know that among the pagans the rulers lord it over them, and their great
26 men make their authority felt. ·This is not to hap-

pen among you. No; anyone who wants to be
27 great among you must be your servant, ·and anyone who wants to be first among you must be
28 your slave, ·just as the Son of Man came not to
be served but to serve, and to give his life as a
ransom for many."
29   As they left Jericho a large crowd followed
30 him. ·Now there were two blind men sitting at
the side of the road. When they heard that it was
Jesus who was passing by, they shouted, "Lord!
31 Have pity on us, Son of David." ·And the crowd
scolded them and told them to keep quiet, but
they only shouted more loudly, "Lord! Have pity
32 on us, Son of David." ·Jesus stopped, called them
over and said, "What do you want me to do for
33 you?" ·They said to him, "Lord, let us have our
34 sight back." ·Jesus felt pity for them and touched
their eyes, and immediately their sight returned
and they followed him.

☩

"Jesus was going up to Jerusalem . . ."—for the
first time, the goal of this fateful trek is named.
Jerusalem, killer of prophets (cf. 23:37), would be the
arena for the remainder of Jesus' ministry. As the capital city looms ahead, a Passion prediction and a final
instruction on discipleship conclude the journey.

The third prediction is the most detailed (20:17–
19). Matthew intensifies the anticipation of the Passion events by explicitly using the word "crucify" (contrast Mark's "put . . . to death," 10:34). The forecast
of death leads into the request of the mother of James
and John (20–23). In Mark's version, the two disciples do their own promotion; Matthew, perhaps to
soften the impression of raw ambition, has their mother

intervene. Their request to share in Jesus' glory "in [his] kingdom" is not rejected but put into perspective. To share his glory, one must be willing to share his pain, to "drink [his] cup" (22). This has been Jesus' constant message in the Gospel (cf. 10:24–25, 38; 16:24). If one sought first the kingdom (accepting its pain and its price), then the Father would provide the rest (6:33).

Neither Zebedee's sons nor the rest of the Twelve would learn quickly to drink from Jesus' cup (26:39–41). So Jesus calls them all together for a final instruction (24–28). True greatness in the community of Jesus is not to be determined by rank or by the flex of power. Greatness is determined by how much one is willing to give in the service of others. This is the kind of love that animated Jesus, the Son of Man, who "came to serve, and to give his life as a ransom for many" (28). Jesus' death, as an act of loving service that brings life to "many," is the ultimate model for genuine discipleship.

Jesus and his followers surge through Jericho, the oasis town a few miles below Jerusalem (29–34). Galilee is far behind. Jesus' instructions to his disciples are practically concluded. His enemies are waiting. It is as if the Gospel hesitates for a moment before plunging into the turbulent events that will end Jesus' life. We are reminded who he is and why he has come. Two blind men sense his presence and cry out in prayer: "Lord! Have pity on us, Son of David" (30, 31). Jesus, the promised Messiah; Jesus, more than Israel had dared hoped; Jesus, who came to heal the blind and to draw believers in his wake.

STUDY QUESTION: Can we really accept the Gospel's
criterion for genuine greatness:
"Anyone who wants to be great
among you must be your servant"?
It is the reverse of most of the
world's way of calculating greatness.

"Jerusalem, Jerusalem"
Final Days in David's City
Matthew 21:1 to 28:20

Matthew 21:1–17
JESUS IS BACK:
THE SON OF DAVID IN THE
JERUSALEM TEMPLE

21 ¹ When they were near Jerusalem and had come in sight of Bethphage on the Mount ² of Olives, Jesus sent two disciples, ·saying to them, "Go to the village facing you, and you will immediately find a tethered donkey and a colt ³ with her. Untie them and bring them to me. ·If anyone says anything to you, you are to say, 'The Master needs them and will send them back ⁴ directly.' " ·This took place to fulfill the prophecy:

⁵ Say to the daughter of Zion:
Look, your king comes to you;
he is humble, he rides on a donkey
and on a colt, the foal of a beast of burden.

⁶ So the disciples went out and did as Jesus had ⁷ told them. ·They brought the donkey and the colt, then they laid their cloaks on their backs ⁸ and he sat on them. ·Great crowds of people spread their cloaks on the road, while others were cutting branches from the trees and spreading them in ⁹ his path. ·The crowds who went in front of him and those who followed were all shouting:

"Hosanna to the Son of David!
Blessings on him who comes in the name of the
   Lord!
Hosanna in the highest heavens!"

10   And when he entered Jerusalem, the whole
city was in turmoil. "Who is this?" people asked,
11 and the crowds answered, "This is the prophet
Jesus from Nazareth in Galilee."
12   Jesus then went into the Temple and drove
out all those who were selling and buying there;
he upset the tables of the money changers and the
13 chairs of those who were selling pigeons. ·"According to scripture," he said, "my house will be
called a house of prayer; but you are turning it
14 into a robber's den." ·There were also blind and
lame people who came to him in the Temple, and
15 he cured them. ·At the sight of the wonderful
things he did and of the children shouting, "Hosanna to the Son of David" in the Temple, the
16 chief priests and the scribes were indignant. ·"Do
you hear what they are saying?" they said to him.
"Yes," Jesus answered, "have you never heard
this:

By the mouths of children, babes in arms,
you have made sure of praise?"

17 With that he left them and went out of the city
to Bethany where he spent the night.

✠

The march from Galilee is over. Jesus and his disciples halt at Bethphage, a village on the eastern crest of
the Mount of Olives, the hill facing Jerusalem across
the Kedron Valley. As Matthew will describe it, the
entry into the capital city is to be dramatic and deliberate. Jesus is David's son; He is King and Messiah; and
he comes back to his city with authority.

"Authority" is a key word in this section of the Gospel. The provocative march into the city, the prophetic gesture of cleansing the Temple, the unflinching facedown with his opponents, and his final, incisive teaching—all of this underlines Jesus' authority as Messiah and Lord. The forces of death are coiled for a strike against Jesus. But death will not erase an impression of absolute authority made in the final days in Jerusalem and its Temple.

The entry into the city is planned (1–5). Two disciples are given crisp orders, and their exacting obedience of these begins to highlight the emphasis on Jesus' authority. The key to the scene is provided by the Old Testament fulfillment text that Matthew introduces into the account (4–5). A blend of Zechariah 9:9 and Isaiah 62:11, the quotation confronts Jerusalem, the "daughter of Zion," with Jesus, her unexpected King. But this King continues to shatter the false expectations of his contemporaries. As the Gospel has consistently portrayed him, Jesus is not regal but humble, a servant of the poor and the outcasts (cf. 12:18). He is not enticed by the equipment of power, but rides on a donkey and a colt, signs of gentleness and peace (cf. Zc 9:10). The reference to *two* animals indicates how exactingly Matthew dresses these events in the authority of the Old Testament. In the original Hebrew quotation, the reference to a "donkey" and a "colt" were synonyms descriptive of a *single* animal. Here they are read as *two,* and Jesus is made to include both in his procession (2, 7).

The crowds, still intrigued by Jesus, are caught up in the triumph of the moment. They decorate the road and, using a verse of Psalm 118:26, explicitly acknowledge Jesus as "Son of David" (9), the Messianic title that prefaced the Gospel (cf. 1:1; 20:30–31). But the chilling hostility that greeted this Son of David at his birth has not been shaken off. Once again (cf. 2:3), Matthew notes that the "whole city" of Jerusalem is disturbed by the news of a king in their midst, and they ask their disbelieving question, "Who is this?" (10). Even the admiring answer of the crowds is not without its portent of death. "This is the prophet Jesus . . ." (11), and Jerusalem, as Jesus will remind his enemies, is a killer of prophets (23:37).

The unlikely royal procession ends at the Temple (12–17). Matthew has thoroughly reworked the chain of events here. In Mark's account (11:11) Jesus enters the Temple only for a brief inspection and then departs until the next day, when he will return to purify it. But in Matthew the purification of the Temple is the final event of Jesus' assertive entry into the City of David.

Only a special currency was accepted for Temple offerings, and for the convenience of pilgrims money changers were available. This commerce was strictly regulated, but the "prophet Jesus" sweeps it from the Temple to make his point about genuine worship (cf. the quote from Is 56:7), just as the prophets of the Old Testament had chosen dramatic signs to shake the conscience of the people. But in Matthew's account Jesus does more. The blind and the lame come to him and he cures them (14). King David had banned such people from entering the house of God (see 2 S 5:8). But now the Temple is thrown open to the outcasts by one who is not only David's "son" but David's "Lord" (cf. 22:41–45) and "greater than the Temple" (12:6).

Reactions once again put the reader of the Gospel on the alert. Children catch the wonder of Jesus (15) and praise the "Son of David." But the religious leaders are "indignant" (16). Jesus squelches their protest with the words of Psalm 8:2. The poor and lowly sense God's power and are not afraid to give thanks for it. With that, Jesus turns and leaves the leaders and the city that they think is theirs.

STUDY QUESTION: The presence of Jesus is like a purging fire, purifying and restoring the Temple. We might place ourselves and our Church in this scene. Are we open to renewal and reform, or do we react with indignation?

PARABLES IN THE TEMPLE

18 As he was returning to the city in the early
19 morning, he felt hungry, ·Seeing a fig tree by the
road he went up to it and found nothing on it
but leaves. And he said to it, "May you never
bear fruit again"; and at that instant the fig tree
20 withered. ·The disciples were amazed when they
saw it. "What happened to the tree," they said,
21 "that it withered there and then?" ·Jesus answered, "I tell you solemnly, if you have faith
and do not doubt at all, not only will you do
what I have done to the fig tree, but even if you
say to this mountain, 'Get up and throw yourself
22 into the sea,' it will be done. ·And if you have
faith, everything you ask for in prayer you will
receive."

23 He had gone into the Temple and was teaching, when the chief priests and the elders of the
people came to him and said, "What authority
have you for acting like this? And who gave you
24 this authority?" ·"And I," replied Jesus, "will ask
you a question, only one; if you tell me the answer to it, I will then tell you my authority for
25 acting like this. ·John's baptism: where did it
come from: heaven or man?" And they argued
it out this way among themselves, "If we say
from heaven, he will retort, 'Then why did you
26 refuse to believe him?'; ·but if we say from man,
we have the people to fear, for they all hold that

27 John was a prophet." ·So their reply to Jesus was,
"We do not know." And he retorted, "Nor will
I tell you my authority for acting like this.

28   "What is your opinion? A man had two sons.
He went and said to the first, 'My boy, you go
29 and work in the vineyard today.' ·He answered,
'I will not go,' but afterward thought better of it
30 and went. ·The man then went and said the same
thing to the second who answered, 'Certainly,
31 sir,' but did not go. ·Which of the two did the
father's will?" "The first," they said. Jesus said
to them, "I tell you solemnly, tax collectors and
prostitutes are making their way into the kingdom
32 of God before you. ·For John came to you, a pattern of true righteousness, but you did not believe
him, and yet the tax collectors and prostitutes did.
Even after seeing that, you refused to think better
of it and believe in him.

33   "Listen to another parable. There was a man,
a landowner, who planted a vineyard; he fenced
it around, dug a winepress in it and built a tower;
then he leased it to tenants and went abroad.
34 When vintage time drew near he sent his servants
35 to the tenants to collect his produce. ·But the
tenants seized his servants, thrashed one, killed
36 another and stoned a third. ·Next he sent some
more servants, this time a larger number, and
37 they dealt with them in the same way. ·Finally he
sent his son to them. 'They will respect my son,'
38 he said. ·But when the tenants saw the son, they
said to each other, 'This is the heir. Come on, let
39 us kill him and take over his inheritance.' ·So
they seized him and threw him out of the vine-
40 yard and killed him. ·Now when the owner of the
vineyard comes, what will he do to those ten-
41 ants?" ·They answered, "He will bring those
wretches to a wretched end and lease the vineyard
to other tenants who will deliver the produce to
42 him when the season arrives." ·Jesus said to
them, "Have you never read in the scriptures:

It was the stone rejected by the builders
that became the keystone.
This was the Lord's doing
and it is wonderful to see?

43
44 I tell you, then, that the kingdom of God will be
taken from you and given to a people who will
produce its fruit."

45   When they heard his parables, the chief priests
and the scribes realized he was speaking about
46 them, ·but though they would have liked to arrest
him they were afraid of the crowds, who looked
on him as a prophet.

1
2 **22** Jesus began to speak to them in parables
once again, ·"The kingdom of heaven may
be compared to a king who gave a feast for his
3 son's wedding. ·He sent his servants to call those
who had been invited, but they would not come.
4 Next he sent some more servants. 'Tell those who
have been invited,' he said, 'that I have my banquet all prepared, my oxen and fattened cattle
have been slaughtered, everything is ready. Come
5 to the wedding.' ·But they were not interested:
one went off to his farm, another to his business,
6 and the rest seized his servants, maltreated them
7 and killed them. ·The king was furious. He dis-
patched his troops, destroyed those murderers
8 and burned their town. ·Then he said to his servants, 'The wedding is ready; but as those who
9 were invited proved to be unworthy, ·go to the
crossroads in the town and invite everyone you
10 can find to the wedding.' ·So these servants went
out on to the roads and collected together everyone they could find, bad and good alike; and the
11 wedding hall was filled with guests. ·When the
king came in to look at the guests he noticed
one man who was not wearing a wedding gar-
12 ment, ·and said to him, 'How did you get in here,
my friend, without a wedding garment?' And the

13 man was silent. ·Then the king said to the attendants, 'Bind him hand and foot and throw him out
into the dark, where there will be weeping and
14 grinding of teeth.' ·For many are called, but few
are chosen."

☩

The day after his triumphant march into Jerusalem,
Jesus returns to the Temple. Matthew will present this
as a day filled with teaching and controversy. On the
way into the city (18–22), Jesus and his disciples
come across a fig tree that bears no fruit. In one of the
Gospel's most bizarre miracles, Jesus curses the barren
tree and it immediately withers. Mark's Gospel had
used this story as a commentary on the fate of the
Temple (cf. 11:12–14, 20–26): On his way to the
purification of the Temple, Jesus curses the tree; on his
return, the tree is found withered. Because Matthew
had Jesus purify the Temple during his first day in
Jerusalem, the story of the fig tree has lost its clear
connection to the fate of the Temple. Now it is used as
an example of the power of determined faith.

Once inside the Temple, Jesus begins to *teach*
(23ff.). But the chief priests and the elders immediately challenge his authority to "act like this," presumably his bold action of the day before and his daring
to teach on their homeground. Jesus' counterquestion
(24–25) unmasks the insincerity of his interrogators
and turns the focus of this entire section to the subject
of recognizing Jesus as the herald of the kingdom.
John the Baptist and Jesus are again paired (cf.
11:1ff.). The leaders failed to recognize John, and
even more tragic, they look with sightless eyes on Jesus
himself.

The three parables that follow pointedly illustrate
the authority of Jesus and the consequences of failing
to recognize it. Each is an easily deciphered allegory, a
type of parable favored by our evangelist in which
every detail is given a symbolic meaning. The parable
of the two sons (28–32) is found only in this Gospel,
and it repeats the demand for repentance verified by
action that is the hallmark of Matthew's Jesus. The
second son knows the right words ("Certainly, sir"),
but his response is hollow. The sadder-but-wiser reaction of the first son is more genuine. He repents and
proves it by action. The point of this parable was already made in the Sermon on the Mount: "It is not
those who say to me, 'Lord, Lord,' who will enter the
kingdom of heaven" (7:21). Jesus now blisters his opponents by turning the parable on them. They did not
hear John's call for repentance and they challenge
Jesus. It is the tax collectors and prostitutes, whose
lives had been a "no" to God, who now repent and
enter the kingdom.

The parable of the wicked husbandman plays the
same melody but with different words (33–46). Israel,
the Lord's vineyard (cf. this traditional image in Is
5:1ff.) is tended by laborers who prove to be faithless.
They reject the servants of the landowner who come to
claim his harvest. Matthew gives heavy clues that these
are the prophets rejected by Israel by describing their
fate as being "killed" and "stoned" (cf. 23:37). Finally the landowner sends his son, the "heir." But the
wicked tenants eject him from the vineyard and kill
him. What will be the fate of people so blind that they
kill the landowner's son? In the words of Psalm
118:22, a favored text of the early Christians, the rejection of Jesus is a rejection of the very cornerstone of

God's kingdom. Matthew draws out the consequences in a verse uniquely his: because Israel has not responded to Jesus and his Gospel, the kingdom is taken from their charge and offered to the gentiles, "who will produce its fruit" (43).

None of these parables is intended to be merely somber commentary on Israel's past failures. The last of the trilogy (22:1–14) makes it clear that these lessons from history are meant to alert Matthew's own Christian community to the consequences of failing to give full and genuine response to the Gospel. The story of a wedding banquet, another traditional biblical metaphor for the kingdom of God, plays out its sad history of refusal. The feast is all prepared but the invited guests are unimpressed. They refuse to come, some going calmly about their business while others turn ugly and kill the servants who announce the feast. The king's reaction is ferocious. The invited guests are punished and their town destroyed. And now the son's wedding feast is thrown open to everyone, "bad and good alike."

So far, so good. Another retelling of Israel's failure to respond to Jesus. The consequences are judgment on Israel (here Matthew may be alluding to the destruction of Jerusalem in A.D. 70, cf. 22:7) and the opening of the kingdom to the gentiles. But the story is not over. The king comes into the banquet hall and finds a guest without a wedding garment (11). Judgment falls on this man, too! He is thrown outside into the darkness. Matthew's message is clear. The Gospel makes the same demand on all, Jew and gentile alike: a life that is "turned around" and given to good deeds. Anything less—an Israel without its harvest, a church without its wedding garment—will be cast into darkness.

STUDY QUESTION: Matthew seems to have a "Catch-22" view of the church: No person or group can be smug about their membership in the Christian community. The test of genuine conversion and a life of good deeds is applied to everyone; everyone can be moved from the "inside" to the outside darkness.

15 Then the Pharisees went away to work out between them how to trap him in what he said.
16 And they sent their disciples to him, together with the Herodians, to say, "Master, we know that you are an honest man and teach the way of God in an honest way, and that you are not afraid of anyone, because a man's rank means nothing to
17 you. ·Tell me your opinion, then. Is it permissible
18 to pay taxes to Caesar or not?" ·But Jesus was aware of their malice and replied, "You hypo-
19 crites! Why do you set this trap for me? ·Let me see the money you pay the tax with." They
20 handed him a denarius, ·and he said, "Whose
21 head is this? Whose name?" ·"Caesar's," they replied. He then said to them, "Very well, give back to Caesar what belongs to Caesar—and to
22 God what belongs to God." ·This reply took them by surprise, and they left him alone and went away.
23 That day some Sadducees—who deny that there is a resurrection—approached him and they
24 put this question to him, ·"Master, Moses said that if a man dies childless, his brother is to marry the widow, his sister-in-law, to raise chil-
25 dren for his brother. ·Now we had case involving seven brothers; the first married and then died without children, leaving his wife to his
26 brother; ·the same thing happened with the sec-

²⁷ ond and third and so on to the seventh, ·and then
²⁸ last of all the woman herself died. ·Now at the
resurrection to which of those seven will she be
wife, since she had been married to them all?"
²⁹ Jesus answered them, "You are wrong, because
you understand neither the scriptures nor the
³⁰ power of God. ·For at the resurrection men and
women do not marry; no, they are like the angels
³¹ in heaven. ·And as for the resurrection of the
dead, have you never read what God himself said
³² to you: ·I am the God of Abraham, the God of
Isaac and the God of Jacob? God is God, not of
³³ the dead, but of the living." ·And his teaching
made a deep impression on the people who heard
it.
³⁴   But when the Pharisees heard that he had si-
³⁵ lenced the Sadducees they got together ·and, to
disconcert him, one of them put a question,
³⁶ "Master, which is the greatest commandment of
³⁷ the Law?" ·Jesus said, "You must love the Lord
your God with all your Heart, with all your soul,
³⁸ and with all your mind. ·This is the greatest and
³⁹ the first commandment. ·The second resembles
⁴⁰ it: You must love your neighbor as yourself. ·On
these two commandments hang the whole Law,
and the Prophets also."
⁴¹   While the Pharisees were gathered around,
⁴² Jesus put to them this question, ·"What is your
opinion about the Christ? Whose son is he?"
⁴³ "David's," they told him. ·"Then how is it," he
said, "that David, moved by the Spirit, calls him
Lord, where he says:

⁴⁴   The Lord said to my Lord:
                Sit at my right hand
                and I will put your enemies
                under your feet?

⁴⁵ "If David can call him Lord, then how can he
⁴⁶ be his son?" ·Not one could think of anything to
say in reply, and from that day no one dared to
ask him any further questions.

☩

Stung by Jesus' parables (21:28 to 22:14), the opponents regroup for a final assault. Three times, they
attempt to ensnare Jesus with contrived questions. But
the Messiah stands in the Temple like an unbeatable
champion and each question is turned back on his enemies until they dare say nothing more (46).

The first wave comes from the Pharisees. They send
their disciples and some supporters of King Herod to
spear Jesus with a politically sensitive dilemma
(15–21): "Is it permissible to pay taxes to Caesar or
not?" Jesus cuts through the hypocrisy of their flatter-
ing words and by asking to see the denarius they "pay
the tax with," reminds them of the solution already
adopted by many Jews. Give to Caesar what belongs to
Caesar, to God what belongs to God. The reply jolts
his questioners, because it nimbly avoids their false dilemma and reasserts Jesus' own teaching. "What belongs to God," the Gospel has insisted, is one's whole
self.

The Sadducees are the next to enter the ring, and
they, too, meet defeat (23–33). These members of the
Temple aristocracy were religious conservatives who
opposed any idea not based strictly on the written
Torah. Thus they attempt to ridicule the doctrine of
bodily resurrection, a relatively recent concept in Judaism, by citing Moses' command about the practice of
Levirite marriage (cf. Dt 25:5f.; Gn 38:8), in which a
man was obliged to have a child by his brother's widow
in order to assure the continuance of the clan. On the
basis of this law, an absurd case about a woman with
seven husbands is posed as a "stopper" for Jesus.

There is no hesitation in his answer. Resurrected life is
not "more of the same" but a *new* life which moves beyond the expectations of the old. Even more serious
than the Sadducees' misunderstanding of resurrection
is the narrowness of their understanding of God. Jesus
matches their citation of Moses by referring to the
words of Yahweh himself (cf. v. 31–32, quoting Ex
3:6). The God of Israel is a "God of the living" whose
fidelity is stronger than death.

The Pharisees huddle together for a last try
(34–40), and a spokesman poses a question about the
greatest commandment of the Law. Jesus' reply is a
summary of his entire teaching in Matthew's Gospel.
The "greatest" commandment is a fusion of two (cf.
Dt 6:5 and Lv 19:18): total, selfless love of God and
neighbor. On this command of love "hang the whole
Law, and the Prophets." Everything God intended in
the Scriptures and in Israel's sacred history finds its
fulfillment in this demand. This is what Jesus had
taught on the mountain in Galilee (cf. 5:17–48;
7:12). This is what his life of obedience to his Father
and gentle compassion to those in need faithfully mir-
rored. And this is what he teaches again as he stands
facing his enemies in the Temple, the religious heart of
Israel.

They have hurled their questions at Jesus and they
have been shattered against his words. Now it is Jesus'
turn: "What is your opinion about the Christ? Whose
son is he?" (41–46). Their reply endorses the title that
has been applied to Jesus throughout this section of the
Gospel: He is David's son. But David's own Psalm (Ps
118:1, a favored text of the early Christians) seems to
imply something more. The Messiah is not only royal
successor to the great David, but he is David's "Lord"

(44). Matthew's Gospel has made this case all along. Jesus is the fulfillment of Israel's great Messianic dream. But he is more. The blind man of Jericho recognized this (20:31), but the religious leaders, too smug in their own wisdom, do not. They turn away discredited and defeated but smoldering with a rage that will soon explode.

STUDY QUESTION: What does it mean to be truly wise? This is the question underlying the scene in the Temple. Jesus is true wisdom, because his divine teaching cuts through the cloying complexities and false dilemmas to the heart of truth, truth summarized by faith in the God of the living and a firm grasp of his command to love.

Matthew 23:1–39
A PROPHET'S RAGE:
"ALAS FOR YOU, SCRIBES
AND PHARISEES"

From the very beginning of the Gospel, Matthew has coupled his majestic portrait of Jesus with a somber record of rejection. Jesus' prophetic teaching in the Temple (see 21:23 to 22:46) had brought the hostility of his enemies to a fast boil. Now Jesus would cauterize this tragic rupture with prophetic words of judgment, scoring the leaders of Israel for their hypocrisy, their blindness, and their narrow legalism. This is the most stark and bitter chapter in the entire Gospel and should be read attentively. Like the rest of the "speeches" of Matthew's Gospel, it is not a transcript of an actual discourse of Jesus but a composite of sayings molded together by the evangelist. Some of the specific issues and the sharp polemical tone of the chapter may reflect not only the altercations between Jesus and his contemporaries but also the later cleavage between the early church and the synagogue (see the Introduction).

The discourse is directed to "the people and his disciples" (1). This is an important clue for properly interpreting the chapter. Jesus' prophetic rage is not meant to be a broken record of accusation against Jewish leaders in the past, but a sober caution for the *Christians* of Matthew's own community about the kinds of attitudes that were fatal to genuine discipleship. Thus this chapter becomes a negative version of the Sermon on the Mount.

GENUINE TEACHERS

1,2 **23** Then addressing the people and his disciples Jesus said, ·"The scribes and the
3 Pharisees occupy the chair of Moses. ·You must
therefore do what they tell you and listen to what
they say; but do not be guided by what they do;
since they do not practice what they preach.
4 They tie up heavy burdens and lay them on men's
shoulders, but will they lift a finger to move
5 them? Not they! ·Everything they do is done to
attract attention, like wearing broader phylacter-
6 ies and longer tassels, ·like wanting to take the
place of honor at banquets and the front seats
7 in the synagogues, ·being greeted obsequiously in
the market squares and having people call them
Rabbi.
8 "You, however, must not allow yourselves to
be called Rabbi, since you have only one Master,
9 and you are all brothers. ·You must call no
one on earth your father, since you have only
10 one Father, and he is in heaven. ·Nor must you
allow yourselves to be called teachers, for you
have only one Teacher, the Christ. The greatest
11 among you must be your servant. ·Anyone who
exalts himself will be humbled, and anyone who
humbles himself will be exalted.

✠

Jesus' opening words reflect the respect for the Law and the institutions of Judaism that has been characteristic of this Gospel (cf. 5:17–20; 10:5–6; 15:24). The scribes and Pharisees were commissioned to teach the Law of Moses, which Jesus came "not to abolish but to complete" (see 5:17). But the words of respect are only preface to the real point of the chapter: a blistering judgment on religious leaders who are hypocritical (10). They are guilty of a fault that Matthew's Gospel has incessantly condemned: not practicing what they preach. Even what they manage to do comes not from the heart but to catch the praise of others.

More is demanded of the disciples of Jesus (8–12). The example and teaching of Jesus and his absolute dedication to the will of the Father—these are the norms of true greatness in the community. Therefore there should be no panting for title and rank. All are brothers, and thus mutual service must be a hallmark of the Christian (cf. 20:24–28).

A PROPHET'S WOES

13   "Alas for you, scribes and Pharisees, you hypocrites! You who shut up the kingdom of heaven
in men's faces, neither going in yourselves nor
allowing others to go in who want to.

15   "Alas for you, scribes and Pharisees, you hypocrites! You who travel over sea and land to make
a single proselyte, and when you have him you
make him twice as fit for hell as you are.

16   "Alas for you, blind guides! You who say, 'If
a man swears by the Temple, it has no force; but
if a man swears by the gold of the Temple, he

17 is bound.' ·Fools and blind! For which is of
greater worth, the gold or the Temple that makes

18 the gold sacred? ·Or else, 'If a man swears by the
altar it has no force; but if a man swears by the

19 offering that is on the altar, he is bound.' ·You
blind men! For which is of greater worth, the
offering or the altar that makes the offering

20 sacred? ·Therefore, when a man swears by the
altar he is swearing by that and by everything on

21 it. ·And when a man swears by the Temple he is
swearing by that and by the One who dwells in

22 it. ·And when a man swears by heaven he is
swearing by the throne of God and by the One
who is seated there.

23   "Alas for you, scribes and Pharisees, you hypocrites! You who pay your tithe of mint and dill

MATTHEW 23:13–32   223

and cummin and have neglected the weightier
matters of the Law—justice, mercy, good faith!
These you should have practiced, without neg-
24 lecting the others. ·You blind guides! Straining
out gnats and swallowing camels!
25   "Alas for you, scribes and Pharisees, you hypocrites! You who clean the outside of cup and
dish and leave the inside full of extortion and
26 intemperance. ·Blind Pharisee! Clean the inside
of cup and dish first so that the outside may become clean as well.
27   "Alas for you, scribes and Pharisees, you hypocrites! You who are like whitewashed tombs
that look handsome on the outside, but inside
are full of dead men's bones and every kind of
28 corruption. ·In the same way you appear to people from the outside like good honest men, but
inside you are full of hypocrisy and lawlessness.
29   "Alas for you, scribes and Pharisees, you hypocrites! You who build the sepulchers of the
prophets and decorate the tombs of holy men,
30 saying, 'We would never have joined in shedding
the blood of the prophets, had we lived in our
31 fathers' day.' ·So! Your own evidence tells against
you! You are the sons of those who murdered the
32 prophets! ·Very well then, finish off the work that
your fathers began.

✠

The sins of the people had wrung from great prophets such as Isaiah (cf. Is 10) and Jeremiah (cf. Jr 20)
strings of "woes" or predictions of doom. The blind
conceit and twisted priorities of the religious leaders
provoke Jesus to the same type of response. And once
again, this list of indictments is not merely to pass
judgment on past generations of Israel's leaders, but to
scorch false leadership in the *Christian* community.

The first four woes (13–24) blister the scribes and Pharisees for their misguided teaching. Instead of leading people toward God's kingdom, they shut the gate (note the contrast to Peter, who holds the keys of the kingdom, 16:19). For a brief time in the first century, there was a robust Jewish missionary effort among the many pagans who admired the beauty of Judaism's ethic. The Gospel sourly predicts that if this mission disseminates the blindness of the leaders, it can lead only to darkness (15). The next two woes specify their failure: The kind of legalism that smothers true religious experience is typified by rabbinic casuistry on oaths (16–22). Out of reverence for God's name, the taker of an oath could swear by something that obliquely referred to God: the Temple, the altar, the heavens. But these euphemisms could be absurd if the oath-taker later denied he meant to swear on God's name. Thus the Gospel cites a number of rabbinic decisions that attempted to control this. But these minute regulations merely paper over a twisted notion of truth. The bond of trust among God's people must be such that a "yes" or a "no" is as firm as an oath (cf. 5:33–37). The leaders' most serious failure is their wrongheaded sense of priorities (23–24). The Jesus of Matthew's Gospel is not an iconoclast; even the law of tithing on one's garden vegetables should be respected. But such details must not be so picked over that they begin to crowd out the truly central and determining obligations of justice and faith. The unflinching demand of Jesus that all the Law be subordinate to the law of love breaks into the Gospel again (cf. 7:14; 22:34–40).

The remaining woes (25–32) settle on a familiar Matthaean refrain: the condemning of disparities between one's heart and one's action. The scribes and Pharisees who fret that a drop of wine on the outside of a sacred vessel might cause ritual impurity are themselves like dishes sparkling on the outside and soiled on the inside (25–26). Or they are like those Palestinian tombs whitewashed annually so no pilgrim would bump into them accidentally and incite an impurity; brilliant on the outside, full of death within (27–28). Purity that counts, Jesus had already insisted, comes from the heart (15:18).

The Jews of Jesus' day were intrigued by the prophets and had built tombs and monuments to honor those who had been mistreated by Israel. But respect for the still voices of the past was costless. Rejection of Jesus showed that the leaders could easily take their place with the generations who had rejected the prophets of old (29–32).

33 "Serpents, brood of vipers, how can you escape
34 being condemned to hell? ·This is why, in my
turn, I am sending you prophets and wise men
and scribes: some you will slaughter and crucify,
some you will scourge in your synagogues and
35 hunt from town to town; ·and so you will draw
down on yourselves the blood of every holy man
that has been shed on earth, from the blood of
Abel Holy to the blood of Zechariah son of
Barachiah whom you murdered between the sanc-
36 tuary and the altar. ·I tell you solemnly, all of
this will recoil on this generation.
37   "Jerusalem, Jerusalem, you that kill the prophets and stone those who are sent to you! How
often have I longed to gather your children, as a
hen gathers her chicks under her wings, and you
38 refused! ·So be it! Your house will be left to you
39 desolate, ·for, I promise, you shall not see me
any more until you say:

Blessings on him who comes in the name of the
Lord!"

☩

The scribes and the Pharisees must bear responsibility for their failure to listen to God's Good News.

Jesus' words of judgment (33) echo John the Baptist's warning at the Jordan (3:7). Rejection of Jesus is a forecast of how his disciples will be treated. The mission discourse of Chapter 10 has already spoken of this, and now this chapter, too, draws to a close with a sober glance to the future. Jesus will send "prophets and wise men and scribes" (34)—characterizations that might describe Jesus himself. But this mission will be rejected, too. So the long line of good people who have suffered in a just cause stretches on from Abel, the first to die in the Bible (Gn 4:10), to the last martyred prophet, Zechariah (the rabbis tended to blend the figure of Zechariah the prophet with the Zechariah of 2 Ch 24:20, the last book in the Hebrew Bible), and now to Jesus (cf. Mt 27:4, 24 when Jesus is referred to as innocent) and into the future. The final words are Jesus' lament over Jerusalem, the city that all Jews love. As Yahweh had brooded over his people to protect them (cf. Is 31:5; Dt 32:11), so this missionary of God longed to do so. But refusal of his mission meant that from now on they would meet him as he comes in judgment (39).

STUDY QUESTION: Jesus' prophetic anger as presented in Matthew's Gospel should be turned not on the Jews (as many Christians have been tempted to do) but on ourselves. The Church must ask if it deserves indictment for hypocrisy, for blindness, for failure to recognize Jesus in the prophets, in the wise men, in the outcasts of our own day.

Matthew 24:1 to 25:46
THE CHURCH FACES ITS FUTURE

As Jesus leaves the Temple, the disciples ask about the fate of this great building. Jesus' blunt prediction of its destruction, and further questions from the disciples (1–3) continue the theme of judgment already sounded in Chapter 23.

Jesus is seated on the Mount of Olives, the broad-shouldered hill that overlooks the Temple. Jewish tradition expected the final judgment to take place on this mountain (see Zc 14:4). Now it provides an apt setting for Jesus' prophetic words about the end of the world and the attitudes the Christian must take in order to be ready for it. As he has done throughout the Gospel, the evangelist assembles the discourse from a variety of materials, including Mark's version of Jesus' final speech (see Mk 13) and some fresh parables.

One of the special features of some sections of this discourse is its so-called "apocalyptic" style, a style popular in Judaism from the second century B.C. to the second century A.D. Because this period of history was so tense, religious writers used a bold and highly symbolic literary style to help steel their readers for a difficult future. As the term "apocalyptic" itself suggests (it comes from a Greek word meaning "reveal"),

writing in this style often took the form of visions in
which a hero or a prophet from the past would forecast
the future (the biblical book of Daniel is a good example). These great visions would include in their predictions some events that the readers would recognize as
already having taken place! This was not meant as
fakery but was a literary device whereby the apocalyptic author could help his audience see this event as a
part of an unfolding historical destiny. Only a few New
Testament writings use an apocalyptic style (see, for
example, The Book of Revelation), but these chapters
from Matthew have some apocalyptic features. Jesus
speaks of the "signs" that will precede the consumma-
tion of the world. Some of these things, for example
the destruction of the Temple and persecution, had already become experiences of Matthew's community.
The reader must now see these traumatic events within
the perspective of the Gospel. Nothing that will befall
the community is outside of God's providence. But responsibility will also continue into the future. The community and its leaders are accountable for their fidelity
or lack of fidelity to the teaching of Jesus.

The discourse, then, is not a clear timetable for the
future. Many of its references to "signs" and significant
events are highly symbolic and, for us at least, very obscure. And Jesus flatly states that no one can predict
the "day and hour" of the end (24:36). This discourse, like all the others, is "gospel," a call for conversion and fidelity as the disciples of Jesus move toward the final victory of God's kingdom.

SIGNS OF FINAL VICTORY

¹ **24** Jesus left the Temple, and as he was going away his disciples came up to draw his at-² tention to the Temple buildings. ·He said to them in reply, "You see all these? I tell you solemnly, not a single stone here will be left on another: ³ everything will be destroyed." ·And when he was sitting on the Mount of Olives the disciples came and asked him privately, "Tell us, when is this going to happen, and what will be the sign of your coming and of the end of the world?"

⁴ And Jesus answered them, "Take care that no ⁵ one deceives you; ·because many will come using my name and saying, 'I am the Christ,' and they ⁶ will deceive many. ·You will hear of wars and rumors of wars; do not be alarmed, for this is something that must happen, but the end will not ⁷ be yet. ·For nation will fight against nation, and kingdom against kingdom. There will be famines ⁸ and earthquakes here and there. ·All this is only the beginning of the birth pangs.

⁹ "Then they will hand you over to be tortured and put to death; and you will be hated by all ¹⁰ the nations on account of my name. ·And then many will fall away; men will betray one another ¹¹ and hate one another. ·Many false prophets will ¹² arise; they will deceive many, ·and with the increase of lawlessness, love in most men will grow

13 cold; ·but the man who stands firm to the end will be saved.

14 "This Good News of the kingdom will be proclaimed to the whole world as a witness to all the nations. And then the end will come.

15 "So when you see the disastrous abomination, of which the prophet Daniel spoke, set up in the
16 Holy Place (let the reader understand), ·then
17 those in Judaea must escape to the mountains; ·if a man is on the housetop, he must not come
18 down to collect his belongings; ·if a man is in the fields, he must not turn back to fetch his
19 cloak. ·Alas for those with child, or with babies
20 at the breast, when those days come! ·Pray that you will not have to escape in winter or on a
21 sabbath. ·For then there will be great distress such as, until now, since the world began, there
22 never has been, nor ever will be again. ·And if that time had not been shortened, no one would have survived; but shortened that time shall be, for the sake of those who are chosen.

23 "If anyone says to you then, 'Look, here is the
24 Christ' or, 'He is there,' do not believe it; ·for false Christs and false prophets will arise and produce great signs and portents, enough to deceive even the chosen, if that were possible.
25 There; I have forewarned you.

26 "If, then, they say to you, 'Look, he is in the desert' do not go there; 'Look, he is in some hid-
27 ing place,' do not believe it; ·because the coming of the Son of Man will be like lightning striking
28 in the east and flashing far into the west. ·Wherever the corpse is, there will the vultures gather.

29 "Immediately after the distress of those days the sun will be darkened, the moon will lose its brightness, the stars will fall from the sky and
30 the powers of heaven will be shaken. ·And then the sign of the Son of Man will appear in heaven; then too all the peoples of the earth will beat their breasts; and they will see the Son of Man coming on the clouds of heaven with power and

31 great glory. ·And he will send his angels with a
loud trumpet to gather his chosen from the four
winds, from one end of heaven to the other.
32   "Take the fig tree as a parable: as soon as its
twigs grow supple and its leaves come out, you
33 know that summer is near. ·So with you when
you see all these things: know that he is near,
34 at the very gates. ·I tell you solemnly, before
this generation has passed away all these things
35 will have taken place. ·Heaven and earth will
pass away, but my words will never pass away."

✠

"When is this going to happen [destruction of the
Temple, see v. 2], and what will be the sign of your
coming?" The way Matthew formulates this lead question (3) indicates an awareness of an indefinite stretch
of time before the final end. The Temple's fate was in
the past; the victorious final coming of Jesus was future. Much of the discourse's organization reflects this
perspective on the end. First there will be remote signs
of the end (4–14), then the beginning of the last days
(15–28), and finally the coming of the Lord (29–31);
in the meantime the community is to be alert and faithful (the point of the judgment parables of 24:36 to
25:30).

The "beginning of the birth pangs" (4–14) will be
marked by wars and persecutions. Even more discon-
certing will be turmoil *within* the community. False
prophets will deceive many, something that may have
been a particular sore point for Matthew's church. And
the teaching of Jesus will be neglected, especially his
law of love (12). But all of this must be seen as "birth
pangs," as part of the great drama of salvation, which

will end in triumph. Jesus' command to "make disciples of all the nations" (see 28:16–20) will be carried out before the end can come (14).

The beginning of the last days (15–28) will bring new portents. The scarring memory of the blasphemy committed in 168 B.C. by the Seleucid ruler Antiochus Ephiphanes is recalled (cf. I M 1:54; Dn 9:27; 11:31; 12:11). He had set up a statue in the Temple sanctuary, and this outrage ignited the Maccabean revolt. The mad Roman emperor Caligula had threatened the same kind of provocation in A.D. 40. This ultimate blasphemy becomes a sign of the agonies to be expected when the end is near. Further evidence of Jewish sensitivity lingers in the Gospel in the detail about the Sabbath (20). The community must pray that the end does not come in the winter nor "on a sabbath," presumably so that escape from the turmoil will not have to violate Sabbath regulations. Once again, false prophets are about their work of deception (23–28). Their enticing words and miraculous powers lead only to false christs. But the final victory is not the preserve of a few. Nor is it something known by the private oracle of select prophets. The coming of the Lord will be as evident as a lightning bolt that flashes from east to west. It will be as inevitable as vultures around a corpse.

The end itself is described with typical apocalyptic imagery (29–35), much of it drawn directly from the Old Testament. The light of sun and moon is tapered and the stars fall from the heavens (cf. Am 8:9). Like a victorious general, the "Son of Man" plants his ensign in the heavens and is greeted with a flourish of trumpets. Some commentators have speculated that the "sign of the Son of Man" might refer to the cross. But

234 FINAL DAYS IN DAVID'S CITY

a vague military metaphor is more probable (see the same imagery in Is 18:3; Jr 4:21; 51:27; it was also used in some Jewish liturgical texts). The moment of judgment is at hand. The Son of Man comes "on the clouds of heaven with power and great glory," a description found in Daniel 7:13–14. And the people of the earth beat their breasts in repentance as they prepare for judgment (cf. Zc 12:10–14).

The use of these traditional metaphors shows that the Gospel does not attempt to provide detailed information about the end. Rather, it affirms its inevitability. The day of judgment will come as surely as the greening of the fig tree is a herald of summer (32). Jesus' own word proclaims that the final days of victory will come. And that word is more sure and more enduring than heaven and earth (cf. 5:18).

36 "But as for that day and hour, nobody knows it, neither the angels of heaven, nor the Son, no one but the Father only.

37 "As it was in Noah's day, so will it be when 38 the Son of Man comes. ·For in those days before the Flood people were eating, drinking, taking wives, taking husbands, right up to the day Noah 39 went into the ark, ·and they suspected nothing till the Flood came and swept all away. It will 40 be like this when the Son of Man comes. ·Then of two men in the fields one is taken, one left; 41 of two women at the millstone grinding, one is taken, one left.

42 "So stay awake, because you do not know the 43 day when your master is coming. ·You may be quite sure of this that if the householder had known at what time of the night the burglar would come, he would have stayed awake and would not have allowed anyone to break through 44 the wall of his house. ·Therefore, you too must stand ready because the Son of Man is coming at an hour you do not expect.

45 "What sort of servant, then, is faithful and wise enough for the master to place him over his household to give them their food at the proper 46 time? ·Happy that servant if his master's arrival 47 finds him at this employment. ·I tell you solemnly, he will place him over everything he

48 owns. ·But as for the dishonest servant who says
49 to himself, 'My master is taking his time,' ·and
sets about beating his fellow servants and eating
50 and drinking with drunkards, ·his master will
come on a day he does not expect and at an hour
51 he does not know. ·The master will cut him off
and send him to the same fate as the hypocrites,
where there will be weeping and grinding of
teeth.

1 25 "Then the kingdom of heaven will be like
this: Ten bridesmaids took their lamps and
2 went to meet the bridegroom. ·Five of them were
3 foolish and five were sensible: ·the foolish ones
did take their lamps, but they brought no oil,
4 whereas the sensible ones took flasks of oil as
5 well as their lamps. ·The bridegroom was late, and
6 they all grew drowsy and fell asleep. ·But at mid-
night there was a cry, 'The bridegroom is here!
7 Go out and meet him.' ·At this, all those brides-
8 maids woke up and trimmed their lamps, ·and the
foolish ones said to the sensible ones, 'Give us
9 some of your oil: our lamps are going out.' ·But
they replied, 'There may not be enough for us
and you; you had better go to those who sell it
10 and buy some for yourselves.' ·They had gone
off to buy it when the bridegroom arrived. Those
who were ready went in with him to the wedding
11 hall and the door was closed. ·The other bridesmaids arrived later. 'Lord, Lord,' they said, 'open
12 the door for us.' ·But he replied, ·I tell you sol-
13 emnly, I do not know you.' ·So stay awake, because you do not know either the day or the
hour.

14   "It is like a man on his way abroad who summoned his servants and entrusted his property
15 to them. ·To one he gave five talents, to another
two, to a third one; each in proportion to his abil-
16 ity. Then he set out. ·The man who had received
the five talents promptly went and traded with

17 them and made five more. ·The man who had re-
18 ceived two made two more in the same way. ·But
the man who had received one went off and dug
a hole in the ground and hid his master's money.
19 Now a long time after, the master of those servants came back and went through his accounts
20 with them. ·The man who had received the five
talents came forward bringing five more. 'Sir,' he
said, 'you entrusted me with five talents; here are
21 five more that I have made.' ·His master said to
him, 'Well done, good and faithful servant; you
have shown you can be faithful in small things,
I will trust you with greater; come and join in
22 your master's happiness.' ·Next the man with the
two talents came forward. 'Sir,' he said, 'you entrusted me with two talents; here are two more
23 that I have made.' ·His master said to him, 'Well
done, good and faithful servant; you have shown
you can be faithful in small things, I will trust
you with greater; come and join in your master's
24 happiness.' ·Last came forward the man who had
the one talent. 'Sir,' said he, 'I had heard you
were a hard man, reaping where you have not
sown and gathering where you have not scat-
25 tered; ·so I was afraid, and I went off and hid
your talent in the ground. Here it is; it was yours,
26 you have it back.' ·But his master answered him,
'You wicked and lazy servant! So you knew that
I reap where I have not sown and gather where I
27 have not scattered? ·Well then, you should have
deposited my money with the bankers, and on
my return I would have recovered my capital
28 with interest. ·So now, take the talent from him
and give it to the man who has the five talents.
29 For to everyone who has will be given more, and
he will have more than enough; but from the
man who has not, even what he has will be
30 taken away. ·As for this good-for-nothing servant,
throw him out into the dark, where there will be
weeping and grinding of teeth.'

✠

Only the Father, not the Son and surely not the disciples, knows the precise hour of the end (36). More important than prediction about the future is how one intends to face it. This concern commands the rest of the discourse.

The story of Noah and the flood (37–41) illustrates how the end can come unexpectedly and find people unprepared. A string of four parables exemplifies the genuine Christian stance. The Christian must be "awake" (the parable of the householder, 42–44, and of the ten virgins, 25:1–13), and of the "faithful" (the parable of the servants, 24:45–51, and the parable of the talents, 25:14–30). By weaving these themes together, Matthew shows that the two qualities are identical. The Christian keeps alert and ready by being faithful to Jesus' teaching. On this basis, an unexpected future holds no terror.

The parable of the householder compares the coming of the Son of Man to a break-in (24:42–44)! If the owner knew when the burglar was coming, he would surely be on guard. The startling comparison is reminiscent of an earlier parable in which Jesus compared himself to the thief who breaks into Satan's household and robs him of his captives (see 12:29). The servant parable (45–51) switches over to the theme of fidelity. The "faithful and wise" servant will be rewarded at the master's return, if he is discovered carrying out his duty of caring for the household. But if the servant should fail in his role of compassion, then he will be punished with the hypocrites.

The parable of the ten virgins is found only in

Matthew (25:1–13). Its story of two very different types of wedding attendants is an allegory on the need for alertness during the indefinite period of time before the end. The foolish bridesmaids are unprepared when the sudden arrival of the groom is announced, and their lack of vigilance costs them access to the wedding celebration. The wise have diligently prepared and are ready for the call. There is some evidence in Jewish writings that "oil" was a symbol of good deeds. If Matthew intended that symbolism here, then he would have neatly blended the two dominant themes of this section. Five of the virgins are wise, because their lives have been filled with good deeds. The lives of the foolish are empty, and thus they are "unknown" to the bridegroom.

The parable of the talents (14–30) continues the emphasis on good use of time, and shuttles back to the theme of fidelity. The "good and faithful" servants are those who are willing to risk their own security in using their gifts well. All are given generous gifts (even one talent is an enormous sum); but not all are willing to use them. The servant entrusted with one talent lets fear smother his initiative, and he must stand accountable before his master. Fear had crippled the fate of the disciples in 8:26, and fear caused Peter to sink into the waves (14:30–31). Once again, Matthew cites fear as the enemy of generous discipleship.

STUDY QUESTION: This section of the Gospel has drawn a lot of attention in recent times. On the basis of this discourse, some confidently forecast the end of the world; while others cite this text as proof of the Gospel's irrelevance. But careful reading of the Gospel challenges both attitudes: it discourages futile speculation about the time of the end and, instead, asks the believer to think seriously about his or her perspective on the destiny of the world. If the future is in God's hands, what should be our own attitude?

JUDGMENT OF THE NATIONS

31 "When the Son of Man comes in his glory, escorted by all the angels, then he will take his
32 seat on his throne of glory. ·All the nations will be assembled before him and he will separate men one from another as the shepherd separates
33 sheep from goats. ·He will place the sheep on his
34 right hand and the goats on his left. ·Then the King will say to those on his right hand, 'Come, you whom my Father has blessed, take for your heritage the kingdom prepared for you since the
35 foundation of the world. ·For I was hungry and you gave me food; I was thirsty and you gave me drink; I was a stranger and you made me wel-
36 come; ·naked and you clothed me, sick and you visited me, in prison and you came to see me.'
37 Then the virtuous will say to him in reply, 'Lord, when did we see you hungry and feed you; or
38 thirsty and give you drink? ·When did we see you a stranger and make you welcome; naked and
39 clothe you; ·sick or in prison and go to see you?'
40 And the King will answer, 'I tell you solemnly, in so far as you did this to one of the least of these brothers of mine, you did it to me.'
41 Next he will say to those on his left hand, 'Go away from me, with your curse upon you, to the eternal fire prepared for the devil and his angels.
42 For I was hungry and you never gave me food; I was thirsty and you never gave me anything to

43 drink; ·I was a stranger and you never made me
welcome, naked and you never clothed me, sick
44 and in prison and you never visited me.' ·Then
it will be their turn to ask, 'Lord, when did we
see you hungry or thirsty, a stranger or naked,
sick or in prison, and did not come to your help?'
45 Then he will answer, ·I tell you solemnly, in so
far as you neglected to do this to one of the
46 least of these, you neglected to do it to me.' ·And
they will go away to eternal punishment, and the
virtuous to eternal life."

✠

We now come to the final phase of the Gospel's
reflection on "judgment." The leaders of Israel have
been judged on their rejection of Jesus (Ch. 23); the
community and its leaders are held accountable for
their fidelity to Jesus' teaching (Chs. 24–25). The "nations," those to whom the mission of the Church is
directed, will be judged on their instinctive response to
the gospel and to those who proclaim it (25:31–46).

This majestic picture of the Son of Man coming as
King to judge the nations and sorting the sheep from
the goats is one of the Gospel's most vivid scenes. Not
only does it portray the moment of judgment in a way
that has stuck in Christian memory, but it also man-
ages a clear distillation of the Gospel message. The
righteous inherit the kingdom because they carry out
the law of love, which is the center of Jesus' teaching
(5:1–48; 7:12; 22:34–40). But there is more. Jesus
himself is identified with the hungry, the stranger, the
poor, the sick, and the oppressed. Three times in
Matthew's Gospel, there is a promise of Jesus' abiding
presence with his church (1:23; 18:20; 28:20). Even
more specifically, he sided with the "little ones" among

the brethren who were entrusted with the ministry of preaching (10:40–42). Both sheep and goats are amazed to discover this. The judgment scene reaffirms in a startling way the criterion for genuine discipleship that has been the hallmark of the Gospel. It is not what one says but what one *does* that counts (cf. 7:21).

By describing the recipients of compassion and the sufferers of neglect as "the least of these brothers of mine" (40, 45), Matthew seems to nudge this judgment scene to another level of meaning. These are the kind of terms used to describe the missionaries. They are brothers, members of the community (cf. 18:15, 21, 35) and the "little ones" who are sent to announce the gospel (cf. 10:42). The "nations," or gentiles, will be judged on how they respond to this Good News. Those who treat these lowly messengers with hospitality and compassion demonstrate that they instinctively grasp the meaning of the gospel.

STUDY QUESTION: As was the case in previous sections of this discourse, the judgment of a specific group becomes a way of proclaiming the meaning of Christian responsibility to all. The question falls to us: How do we respond to the poor and "insignificant" people of our time? Do we recognize in them Jesus and his Good News?

PRELUDE TO THE PASSION STORY

¹ ² **26** Jesus had now finished all he wanted to say, and he told his disciples, ·"It will be Passover, as you know, in two days time, and the Son of Man will be handed over to be crucified."

³ Then the chief priests and the elders of the people assembled in the palace of the high priest, ⁴ whose name was Caiaphas, ·and made plans to arrest Jesus by some trick and have him put to ⁵ death. ·They said, however, "It must not be during the festivities; there must be no disturbance among the people."

⁶ Jesus was at Bethany in the house of Simon the ⁷ leper, when ·a woman came to him with an alabaster jar of the most expensive ointment, and ⁸ poured it on his head as he was at table. ·When they saw this, the disciples were indignant. "Why ⁹ this waste?" they said. ·"This could have been sold at a high price and the money given to the poor." ¹⁰ Jesus noticed this. "Why are you upsetting the woman?" he said to them. "What she has done ¹¹ for me is one of the good works indeed! ·You have the poor with you always, but you will not ¹² always have me. ·When she poured this ointment on my body, she did it to prepare me for burial. ¹³ I tell you solemnly, wherever in all the world this

Good News is proclaimed, what she has done will
be told also, in remembrance of her."

14   Then one of the Twelve, the man called Judas
15   Iscariot, went to the chief priests ·and said,
"What are you prepared to give me if I hand him
16   over to you?" ·They paid him thirty silver pieces,
and from that moment he looked for an opportunity to betray him.

☖

The great drama of Jesus' Passion begins with the
same kind of transitional statement that occurred after
each of the major discourses of the Gospel (cf. above,
7:28). But now Jesus has finished "all" his speeches;
the Passover, the moment of Jesus' final decisive action, has arrived. The first sixteen verses of the Passion
story serve as a prelude to the quick-paced narrative
that will follow; the main protagonists are brought on
stage, the issues are drawn, and the forces that will ultimately bring the story to its climax are set in motion.

Unlike Mark, whose Passion story has an abrupt beginning, Matthew chooses to open with a rather formal
scene. Jesus once more predicts his approaching death.
The same Son of Man who will come in victorious
judgment at the end of the world (25:31–46) must
first experience the agony of defeat and death. Both
dimensions—death and victory—are essential to the
gospel portrait of Jesus. The way Matthew shapes
these opening verses is reminiscent of Deuteronomy
32:45, where Moses completes his instructions to the
people of Israel and moves to his death on Mount
Nebo. Jesus, the new Moses, has completed his teaching, and now with measured assurance he confronts his
death.

Throughout the Gospel, and even here at a moment of humiliation and death, Matthew views Jesus through the lens of resurrection. Jesus, the suffering Son of Man, is also the risen Lord of glory. This sets off a series of vivid contrasts that begins in the prelude and continues into the Passion story. Jesus calmly predicts his impending death, while the chief priests furtively plot against him (3–5). Jesus welcomes the kindness of an unknown woman (6–13); then one of the Twelve barters away his master (14–15). Such counterpoints are designed to highlight Jesus' majesty and, at the same time, to offer forceful object lessons for the disciples.

The circumstances of Jesus' death would necessitate a hasty burial (see 27:57–61). But the kindness of an unknown woman at Bethany makes sure that Jesus' body is not denied the loving respect that Judaism showed for its dead (6–13). Jesus interprets her action as his burial anointing. The disciples protest, because they have not as yet fully comprehended Jesus' teaching. This woman's generous act of compassion in response to an immediate need is what the gospel is all about (13; cf. 25:31–46).

The mood darkens. Judas, pointedly identified as "one of the Twelve," goes to the chief priests to betray Jesus. Throughout the Passion story, Matthew remains amazingly faithful to the text of Mark, but he does like to add snatches of dialogue, as in this scene with Judas (15; cf. Mk 14:10). The thirty silver pieces is an evident allusion to Zechariah 11:12. The significance of this text for Matthew will be spelled out in 27:3–10, where the Judas story comes to its tragic finale. The frequent but subtle Old Testament allusions in the Passion story signal to the readers that even these bleak moments have not escaped God's providence.

The prelude closes on a haunting note. "From that moment" (the same emphatic time phrase used in 4:17, cf. 16:21), Judas looks for an "opportunity" to betray Jesus. In 26:18, the same root word, *kairos,* an "opportune time," is found on the lips of Jesus. Both men move toward the *kairos*: one toward death but ultimate victory, the other toward seeming victory but ultimate death.

STUDY QUESTION: Throughout the Gospel, the evangelist has insisted on the role of suffering in Jesus' life. Now that drama will be played out in detail. How do suffering and death fit into my life? Do I face this fundamental question, or do I try to wink it away?

FELLOWSHIP AND BETRAYAL:
JESUS' LAST MEAL WITH HIS DISCIPLES

17 Now on the first day of Unleavened Bread the disciples came to Jesus to say, "Where do you want us to make the preparations for you to eat 18 the passover?" ·"Go to so-and-so in the city," he replied, "and say to him, 'The Master says: My time is near. It is at your house that I am keep- 19 ing Passover with my disciples.' " ·The disciples did what Jesus told them and prepared the pass- over.

20 When evening came he was at table with the 21 twelve disciples. ·And while they were eating he said, "I tell you solemnly, one of you is about to 22 betray me." ·They were greatly distressed and started asking him in turn, "Not I, Lord, surely?" 23 He answered, "Someone, who has dipped his 24 hand into the dish with me, will betray me. ·The Son of Man is going to his fate, as the scriptures say he will, but alas for that man by whom the Son of Man is betrayed! Better for that man if he 25 had never been born!" ·Judas, who was to betray him, asked in his turn, "Not I, Rabbi, surely?" "They are your own words," answered Jesus.

26 Now as they were eating, Jesus took some bread, and when he had said the blessing he broke it and gave it to the disciples. "Take it and 27 eat"; he said, "this is my body." ·Then he took a

cup, and when he had returned thanks he gave it
to them. "Drink all of you from this," he said,
28 "for this is my blood, the blood of the convenant,
which is to be poured out for many for the for-
29 giveness of sins. ·From now on, I tell you, I shall
not drink wine until the day I drink the new wine
with you in the kingdom of my Father."
30   After psalms had been sung they left for the
31 Mount of Olives. ·Then Jesus said to them, "You
will all lose faith in me this night, for the scripture says: I shall strike the shepherd and the
32 sheep of the flock will be scattered, ·but after my
33 resurrection I shall go before you to Galilee." ·At
this, Peter said, "Though all lose faith in you, I
34 will never lose faith." ·Jesus answered him, "I
tell you solemnly, this very night, before the cock
crows, you will have disowned me three times."
35 Peter said to him, "Even if I have to die with
you, I will never disown you." And all the disciples said the same.

☩

The Passion story turns out to be a proving ground
for fidelity. Jesus himself is the model; he faces suffering and death with the same integrity and obedience
that marked his life. Other characters in the Passion
account—the disciples, the Jewish leaders, the Romans
—are far less than model. Their infidelity demonstrates
how fragile discipleship can be. This concern becomes
clear in the way the account of the Last Supper unfolds. This moment of intense union between Jesus and
the Twelve is framed with predictions of Judas' betrayal, Peter's denial, and the disciples' desertion.

Preparations for the Passover meal set the tone
(17–19). Matthew concentrates on Jesus' crisp commands and the disciples' intent obedience. His "time is
near" (18); preparation must begin. When everything

is ready, Jesus and his twelve disciples gather for the
Passover meal. Prediction of Judas' treachery (20–25)
turns the mood sober. Sharing the same dish, a gesture of friendship, marks Judas as the betrayer. Judas'
words (25), "Not I, Rabbi?" use a title for Jesus that
the Gospel has discouraged (23:8) and stand in sharp
contrast with the majestic title used by the rest of the
disciples: "Not I, *Lord*" (22). Jesus' reply confirms
Judas' unwitting confession of guilt (25).

The ritual of the supper is succinctly narrated. The
concentration on Jesus' words over the bread and wine
reflects the use of this text in the Church's liturgy. In
this fellowship meal shared by Jesus and his disciples,
the Church recognizes the foundation of its Eucharist.
Not only is Jesus' death an inauguration of the new
covenant promised by Jeremiah (Jr 31:31–34), and
not only is it a dying "for the sake of many," as
Isaiah's suffering servant had prefigured (cf. Is 53:12),
but this death is "for the forgiveness of sins." This latter phrase, added by Matthew, recalls what the Gospel
had previously affirmed about Jesus: He is the savior
who frees the people from their sins (1:21); he is the
servant who lifts the burden of pain and death from the
helpless (8:17; 12:18) and who gives his life in service for the many (20:28). This Jesus is the very one
whose death is proclaimed as the final act of love
which forgives the world's sin and frees those trapped
in the vise of death (cf. 27:51–54).

The account ends on a note of triumph (29). The
pledge of unity symbolized in the Eucharist cannot be
broken, even by death. The next celebration between
Jesus and his disciples will be with the new wine of the
kingdom.

But the darkness of the Passion story is only momentarily dissipated. Jesus uses the words of Zechariah 13:7 to predict that the disciples and Peter will "lose faith" (literally, be "scandalized in me"; for the significance of the word, cf. above 18:6). Ultimate reconciliation is promised after the resurrection (32); but, for now, the disciples are not "alert," and they fail to take Jesus' warning to heart.

STUDY QUESTION: The Gospel surrounds Christianity's sacred celebration of unity and hope with examples of weakness and infidelity. What does this suggest about the meaning of the Eucharist?

PRAYER AND ARREST IN THE GARDEN

36 Then Jesus came with them to a small estate called Gethsemane; and he said to his disciples,
37 "Stay here while I go over there to pray." ·He took Peter and the two sons of Zebedee with him. And sadness came over him, and great distress.
38 Then he said to them, "My soul is sorrowful to the point of death. Wait here and keep awake
39 with me." ·And going on a little further he fell on his face and prayed. "My Father," he said, if it is possible, let this cup pass me by. Never-
40 theless, let it be as you, not I, would have it." ·He came back to the disciples and found them sleeping, and he said to Peter, "So you had not the
41 strength to keep awake with me one hour? ·You should be awake, and praying not to be put to the test. The spirit is willing, but the flesh is
42 weak." ·Again, a second time, he went away and prayed: "My Father," he said, "if this cup cannot pass by without my drinking it, your will be
43 done!" ·And he came back again and found them
44 sleeping, their eyes were so heavy. ·Leaving them there, he went away again and prayed for the
45 third time, repeating the same words. ·Then he came back to the disciples and said to them, "You can sleep on now and take your rest. Now the hour has come when the Son of Man is to be

46 betrayed into the hands of sinners. ·Get up! Let us go! My betrayer is already close at hand."

47 He was still speaking when Judas, one of the Twelve, appeared, and with him a large number of men armed with swords and clubs, sent by the

48 chief priests and elders of the people. ·Now the traitor had arranged a sign with them. "The one I kiss," he had said, "he is the man. Take him in

49 charge." ·So he went straight up to Jesus and

50 said, "Greetings, Rabbi," and kissed him. ·Jesus said to him, "My friend, do what you are here for." Then they came forward, seized Jesus and

51 took him in charge. ·At that, one of the followers of Jesus grasped his sword and drew it; he struck out at the high priest's servant, and cut off his ear.

52 Jesus then said, "Put your sword back, for all who

53 draw the sword will die by the sword. ·Or do you think that I cannot appeal to my Father who would promptly send more than twelve legions of

54 angels to my defence? ·But then, how would the scriptures be fulfilled that say this is the way it

55 must be?" ·It was at this time that Jesus said to the crowds, "Am I a brigand, that you had to set out to capture me with swords and clubs? I sat teaching in the Temple day after day and you

56 never laid hands on me." ·Now all this happened to fulfill the prophecies in scripture. Then all the disciples deserted him and ran away.

☩

The scene shifts to Gethsemane, a quiet grove on the slopes of the Mountain of Olives, where the "hand-[ing] over," that nightmare moment predicted three times in the Gospel (17:22; 20:18; 26:2), is about to come true. The moment is preceded by a period of intense prayer (36–44), a scene that has made its impact on all four Gospels and even the Epistle to the Hebrews (5:7–9) and which reveals, in startling baldness, Jesus' humanity. He fears death and pleads to be delivered from it.

Jesus takes a select trio of disciples with him (36). This opening verse seems to evoke deliberately Gn 22:5, where Abraham leaves his servants behind and takes Isaac to the place of sacrifice. Once again, the obedience of an Israelite will be tested, this time God's own Son. In Mark's account, emphasis falls on the failure of the disciples, as Jesus comes three times to find them asleep. Matthew shifts the focus to Jesus' three-fold prayer (39, 42, 44), seeking, even in the midst of fear and isolation, to do the will of his Father. In verse 42, Matthew adds the phrase, "your will be done," a direct quotation from the prayer he had previously taught his disciples (6:10). Jesus does what he teaches.

His faithful prayer has its effect. Jesus rises up with renewed strength to face his hour (46). The disciples, like the sluggish householder and the unwise servants (see 24:42–51), are unprepared for this moment of truth. They will flee; but Jesus will stand fast.

That moment comes with Judas and an armed band. Judas has found the "opportune time" he has been seeking (26:16). Matthew's fascination with the fallen disciple continues, as once again he adds dialogue to the Marcan story (cf. above 26:15, 25). The betrayer kisses Jesus and hails him once more with the inadequate title "Rabbi." Jesus' reply hints at the ultimate victory in which the Gospel views all these events. He is well aware of Judas' intention, and only after Jesus has thus signaled his "permission" can the armed band seize him (50).

One of Jesus' followers (the Gospel of John

identifies him as Peter) makes a futile attempt at resistance by striking the high priest's servant. Matthew makes this another opportunity for exemplifying Jesus' obedience. In the Sermon on the Mount, Jesus demanded love of enemies (5:44) and eschewed all retaliation (5:39). He maintains that teaching now, as violent hands lash out at him (52–54). No one—neither his tattered band of followers nor legions of angel warriors—should make Jesus swerve from his way of obedience. Jesus rejected the seduction of miraculous intervention in the desert (cf. 4:1–11), and he rejects it here. God's will expressed in the Scriptures must be fulfilled (54, 56).

The disciples flee, and Jesus is abandoned to those who seek to destroy him (56). Now the Passion story will run its swift course to the cross.

STUDY QUESTION: Jesus struggles to be faithful in the midst of suffering and confusion. What does this scene teach us about the meaning of genuine Christian prayer?

THE VERDICT OF THE SANHEDRIN:
HE DESERVES TO DIE

57 The men who had arrested Jesus led him off to Caiaphas the high priest, where the scribes and 58 the elders were assembled. ·Peter followed him at a distance, and when he reached the high priest's palace, he went in and sat down with the attendants to see what the end would be.

59 The chief priests and the whole Sanhedrin were looking for evidence against Jesus, however false, on which they might pass the death sentence. 60 But they could not find any, though several lying witnesses came forward. Eventually two stepped 61 forward ·and made a statement, "This man said, 'I have power to destroy the Temple of God and 62 in three days build it up.' " ·The high priest then stood up and said to him, "Have you no answer to that? What is this evidence these men are 63 bringing against you?" ·But Jesus was silent. And the high priest said to him, "I put you on oath by the living God to tell us if you are the Christ, 64 the Son of God." ·"The words are your own," answered Jesus. "Moreover, I tell you that from this time onward you will see the Son of Man seated at the right hand of the Power and coming 65 on the clouds of heaven." ·At this, the high priest tore his clothes and said, "He has blasphemed. What need of witnesses have we now?

66 There! You have just heard the blasphemy. ·What is your opinion?" They answered, "He deserves to die."

67 Then they spat in his face and hit him with
68 their fists; others said as they struck him, ·"Play the prophet, Christ! Who hit you then?"

69 Meanwhile Peter was sitting outside in the courtyard, and a servant girl came up to him and said, "You too were with Jesus the Galilean."
70 But he denied it in front of them all. "I do not know what you are talking about," he said.
71 When he went out to the gateway another servant girl saw him and said to the people there,
72 "This man was with Jesus the Nazarene." ·And again, with an oath, he denied it, "I do not know
73 the man." ·A little later the bystanders came up and said to Peter, "You are one of them for sure!
74 Why, your accent gives you away." ·Then he started calling down curses on himself and swearing, "I do not know the man." At that moment
75 the cock crew, ·and Peter remembered what Jesus had said, "Before the cock crows you will have disowned me three times." And he went outside and wept bitterly.

1 27 When morning came, all the priests and the elders of the people met in council to
2 bring about the death of Jesus. ·They had him bound, and led him away to hand him over to Pilate the governor.

3 When he found that Jesus had been condemned, Judas his betrayer was filled with remorse and took the thirty silver pieces back to
4 the chief priests and elders. ·"I have sinned," he said; "I have betrayed innocent blood." "What is that to us?" they replied. "That is your concern."
5 And flinging down the silver pieces in the sanctuary he made off, and went and hanged himself.
6 The chief priests picked up the silver pieces and said, "It is against the Law to put this into the
7 treasury; it is blood money." ·So they discussed

the matter and bought the potter's field with it as
8 a graveyard for foreigners, ·and this is why the
9 field is called the Field of Blood today. ·The
words of the prophet Jeremiah were then fulfilled: And they took the thirty silver pieces, the
sum at which the precious One was priced by
10 the children of Israel, ·and they gave them for the
potter's field, just as the Lord directed me.

☩

Jesus, now a prisoner, is taken from the garden to
the palace of Caiaphas, the high priest. Here the Jewish leaders will assemble to confront Jesus with their
charges. None of the evangelists presents this scene
with the precision of court transcripts. In fact the historical details of these proceedings are almost impossible to reconstruct. For the Gospels, this moment is another opportunity to reflect on who Jesus is and what it
means to be his disciple.

Matthew uses Mark's device of a dramatic pairing of
Jesus and Peter (57–75). While Jesus unflinchingly
proclaims his identity as Messiah, Son of God, and Son
of Man, Peter recoils in fear and denies that he is a disciple of Jesus.

The hearing before the Sanhedrin, the official ruling
body of Judaism, moves swiftly (59–68). A parade of
false witnesses prove futile. But finally two witnesses
(the number demanded for valid testimony according
to Dt 19:15) accuse Jesus of proclaiming power over
the Jerusalem Temple (61). The Gospel does not
brand this allegation as false, because it knows that
Jesus is indeed "one greater than the Temple" and
"master of the sabbath" (see Mt 12:6–8). Jesus' only
answer is a majestic silence (a trait reminiscent of the

suffering servant in Is 53:7). Then the solemn moment comes. The high priest asks Jesus under oath if he is "the Christ, the Son of God" (63). But the high priest is an unbelieving accuser, and thus Jesus' answer confirms the truth of Caiaphas' words at the same time it indicts his lack of faith. Jesus is the Christ and the Son of God, but he is also the exalted "Son of Man," who will come in triumph to judge the world. Even *now* ("from this time onward"), in Jesus' impending death, God's victory has begun (cf. 27:51-54).

Reaction to Jesus' words is predictable. As the Gospel story had already demonstrated, Jesus is rejected by his own. He is judged deserving of death (66), and with blows and insults, the leaders mock Jesus' claim to be the "Christ."

The scene now shifts to Peter (69-75), who at the beginning of the hearing had been sitting and watching —as the Gospel story notes with gentle irony—"to see what the end would be." Peter will not see the end because, as Jesus predicted (26:30-35), the leader of the Twelve will fail. Matthew continues to make Peter an object lesson in discipleship. Fear forces Peter to escalate his denials from evasion to an oath (expressly forbidden by Jesus in 5:34) to cursing and swearing that he does "not know the man" (74). But in spite of his denial, Peter the Galilean is one of those "with Jesus the Nazarene." And when the predicted cockcrow (see 26:34) pierces the night, Peter illustrates true conversion: he remembers the word of Jesus and weeps tears of repentance (75).

The night-long session of the Sanhedrin concludes with a death verdict for Jesus and a resolution to take him to Pilate, the Roman governor of Judea and the only one empowered to carry out capital punishment

(27:1–2). At this point Matthew interrupts the narrative to conclude the tragic history of another disciple, Judas (3–10). Matthew's version of Judas' death (cf. an alternate story in Acts 1:18) is an intricate blend of Old Testament allusions and some of the consistent themes of his Gospel. As predicted (26:20–25), Judas' betrayal leads to death. He is not moved to repentance but only to remorse and despair. But the responsibility of rejecting Jesus does not end with Judas. The chief priests pick up the "blood money" Judas had flung into the Temple and thus symbolize that they, too, must bear responsibility for their lack of faith. Matthew views this entire episode from the viewpoint of the Old Testament. The words of Zechariah 11:12–13 (cf. Mt 27:9–10) had predicted such betrayal. But it is Jeremiah whose symbol of the potter (Jr Chs. 18 and 32) and of a burial field (Jr 19) provide Matthew with the atmosphere of judgment cast over this tragic episode. As with all the fulfillment texts, Matthew affirms that these events fall within the context of God's mysterious providence.

STUDY QUESTION: Three Galileans face their moment of truth: Judas, Peter, Jesus. The Gospel subtly prods us—where do we stand?

THE VERDICT OF PILATE AND THE PEOPLE: "LET HIM BE CRUCIFIED"

11 Jesus, then, was brought before the governor, and the governor put to him this question, "Are you the king of the Jews?" Jesus replied, "It is
12 you who say it." ·But when he was accused by the chief priests and the elders he refused to an-
13 swer at all. ·Pilate then said to him, "Do you not hear how many charges they have brought against
14 you?" ·But to the governor's complete amazement, he offered no reply to any of the charges.

15 At festival time it was the governor's practice to release a prisoner for the people, anyone they
16 chose. ·Now there was at that time a notorious
17 prisoner whose name was Barabbas. ·So when the crowd gathered, Pilate said to them, "Which do you want me to release for you: Barabbas, or
18 Jesus who is called Christ?" ·For Pilate knew it was out of jealousy that they handed him over.

19 Now as he was seated in the chair of judgment his wife sent him a message, "Have nothing to do with that man; I have been upset all day by a dream I had about him."

20 The chief priests and the elders, however, had persuaded the crowd to demand the release of
21 Barabbas and the execution of Jesus. ·So when the governor spoke and asked them, "Which of the two do you want me to release for you?" they

22 said, "Barabbas." ·"But in that case," Pilate said
   to them, "what am I to do with Jesus who is
   called Christ?" They all said, "Let him be cruci-
23 fied!" ·"Why?" he asked. "What harm has he
   done?" But they shouted all the louder, "Let him
24 be crucified!" ·Then Pilate saw that he was making no impression, that in fact a riot was immi-
   nent. So he took some water, washed his hands in
   front of the crowd and said, "I am innocent of
25 this man's blood. It is your concern." ·And the
   people to a man, shouted back, "His blood be
26 on us and on our children!" ·Then he released
   Barabbas for them. He ordered Jesus to be first
   scourged and then handed over to be crucified.
27   The governor's soldiers took Jesus with them
   into the Praetorium and collected the whole co-
28 hort around him. ·Then they stripped him and
29 made him wear a scarlet cloak, ·and having
   twisted some thorns into a crown they put this
   on his head and placed a reed in his right hand.
   To make fun of him they knelt to him saying,
30 "Hail, king of the Jews!" ·And they spat on him
   and took the reed and struck him on the head
31 with it. ·And when they had finished making fun
   of him, they took off the cloak and dressed him
   in his own clothes and led him away to crucify
   him.

☩

It is now Pilate's turn to decide Jesus' fate. The
Roman trial scene will closely parallel the account of
the hearing before the Sanhedrin. The basic structure is
the same: interrogation, verdict, mockery. And as in
the previous scene, the evangelist is more interested in
significance than in detailed information.

Pilate's opening question, "Are you the king of the

Jews?" (11), strikes the theme of Jesus' Messiahship sounded earlier by Caiaphas (26:63). The title "king of the Jews" emphasizes the political overtones of Jewish Messianic hopes. Once again, Jesus' answer is deliberately enigmatic: he confirms the truth of Pilate's words but recognizes that the governor is unaware of what he has stated. The Jewish leaders add a chorus of accusations, but Jesus, God's Servant (cf. Is 53:7), reverts to his eloquent silence.

Pilate is baffled by his prisoner and attempts to secure his release through a custom attested only in the Gospels, the freeing of a prisoner as a gesture of benevolence during the great Jewish season of Passover. Matthew uses this information, already provided by Mark, as a means of sharpening the underlying issue of the trial: one must accept or reject Jesus as the Christ. The choice is posed in verse 17 and again in verse 21. The drama of the choice is heightened by preparation. Pilate's wife has been warned in a dream (always a medium of divine messages in Matthew's Gospel, cf. Ch. 2) that Jesus is innocent and pleads with her husband on his behalf (19). Meanwhile the leaders sway the crowds for Barabbas. In some very ancient manuscripts, Barabbas' name is given as *"Jesus* Barabbas." If this was the original wording, then the choice is posed even more dramatically: "Who is to be released? Jesus Barabbas or Jesus the Christ?" Crowd and leaders become one and demand that Jesus be crucified.

Matthew seals a dramatic choice with dramatic gestures (24–25): Pilate, the Roman governor, washes his hands, using an Old Testament ritual that declares one innocent of murdered blood (cf. Dt 21:6f.). The

crowds, now designated by the corporate title "the people" (25), use another Old Testament formula, which
is a declaration of responsibility: "His blood be on us
and on our children" (cf. 1 K 2:32f.). This passage
should not be constructed as a foundation for anti-
Semitism. Matthew himself was probably a Jew, and
his own church certainly included a substantial proportion of Jews. Thus this gospel incident could not be intended as a condemnation of the Jewish people.
Matthew makes it a solemn declaration because he recognizes here a pivotal moment in salvation history. In
the paradox of God's providence, the promise of salvation, which had been confined to Israel, was now,
through the death and resurrection of Jesus, to break
out into the whole world. The ones who rejected Jesus
would have to bear responsibility for their choice.
Matthew's church may have interpreted the destruction
of the Temple in A.D. 70 as fulfilling the time span of
27:25: "on us and on our children," i.e. on the contemporaries of Jesus and the following generation.
From now on, the Gospel's promise of forgiveness and
new life would be open to all who would respond (cf.
Mt 21:43).

Mockery and insult conclude the trial (27–31).
Jesus' claim to kingship is cruelly parodied by the soldiers. Another moment of deep irony lies beneath the
surface of the narrative. The reader knows that Jesus *is*
King, a King who rejects the trappings of royalty
ridiculed by the soldiers (cf. 21:5). This macabre cor-
onation is unwitting preparation for Jesus' greatest act
of service, and it is service that is the real basis of
Jesus' power (cf. 20:28).

STUDY QUESTION: The evangelist searches history and discovers God's providence even in the midst of tragedy and failure. We should search the history of our own significant life choices, and place them in the perspective of faith.

Matthew 27:32–66
THE DEATH OF GOD'S SON
AND THE BEGINNING OF THE NEW AGE

32 On their way out, they came across a man
from Cyrene, Simon by name, and enlisted him
33 to carry his cross. ·When they had reached a
place called Golgotha, that is, the place of the
34 skull, ·they gave him wine to drink mixed with
35 gall, which he tasted but refused to drink. ·When
they had finished crucifying him they shared out
36 his clothing by casting lots, ·and then sat down
and stayed there keeping guard over him.

37 Above his head was placed the charge against
him; it read: "This is Jesus, the King of the
38 Jews." ·At the same time two robbers were crucified with him, one on the right and one on the
left.

39 The passers-by jeered at him; they shook their
40 heads ·and said, "So you would destroy the Temple and rebuild it in three days! Then save yourself! If you are God's son, come down from the
41 cross!" ·The chief priests with the scribes and
42 elders mocked him in the same way. ·"He saved
others," they said, "he cannot save himself. He is
the king of Israel; let him come down from the
43 cross now, and we will believe in him. ·He puts
his trust in God; now let God rescue him if he
wants him. For he did say, 'I am the son of

⁴⁴ God.' " ·Even the robbers who were crucified with him taunted him in the same way.

⁴⁵ From the sixth hour there was darkness over
⁴⁶ all the land until the ninth hour. ·And about the ninth hour, Jesus cried out in a loud voice, "Eli, Eil, lama sabachthani?" that is, "My God, my
⁴⁷ God, why have you deserted me?" ·When some of those who stood there heard this, they said, "The
⁴⁸ man is calling on Elijah," ·and one of them quickly ran to get a sponge which he dipped in vinegar and, putting it on a reed, gave it him to
⁴⁹ drink. ·"Wait!" said the rest of them, "and see
⁵⁰ if Elijah will come to save him." ·But Jesus, again crying out in a loud voice, yielded up his spirit.

⁵¹ At that, the veil of the Temple was torn in two from top to bottom; the earth quaked; the rocks
⁵² were split; ·the tombs opened and the bodies of
⁵³ many holy men rose from the dead, ·and these, after his resurrection, came out of the tombs, entered the Holy City and appeared to a number
⁵⁴ of people. ·Meanwhile the centurion, together with the others guarding Jesus, had seen the earthquake and all that was taking place, and they were terrified and said, "In truth this was a son of God."

⁵⁵ And many women were there, watching from a distance, the same women who had followed Jesus
⁵⁶ from Galilee and looked after him. ·Among them were Mary of Magdala, Mary the mother of James and Joseph, and the mother of Zebedee's sons.

⁵⁷ When it was evening, there came a rich man of Arimathaea, called Joseph, who had himself be-
⁵⁸ come a disciple of Jesus. ·This man went to Pilate and asked for the body of Jesus. Pilate thereupon
⁵⁹ ordered it to be handed over. ·So Joseph took the
⁶⁰ body, wrapped it in a clean shroud ·and put it in his own tomb which he had hewn out of the rock. He then rolled a large stone across the entrance

⁶¹ of the tomb and went away. ·Now Mary of Magdala and the other Mary were there, sitting opposite the sepulcher.

⁶² Next day, that is, when Preparation Day was over, the chief priests and the Pharisees went in ⁶³ a body to Pilate ·and said to him, "Your Excellency, we recall that this impostor said, while he was still alive, 'After three days I shall rise ⁶⁴ again.' ·Therefore give the order to have the sepulcher kept secure until the third day, for fear his disciples come and steal him away and tell the people, 'He has risen from the dead.' This last piece of fraud would be worse than what went before." ⁶⁵ ·"You may have your guard," said Pilate to them. "Go and make all as secure as you know ⁶⁶ how." ·So they went and made the sepulcher secure, putting seals on the stone and mounting a guard.

✠

With this scene Matthew reaches the climax of the entire gospel story. Jesus will die, but through that death astounding new life will begin.

At Golgotha, the execution site outside Jerusalem, Jesus is offered a mild sedative, stripped of his clothing, and crucified (32–38). The offering of wine and gall and the casting of lots for Jesus' garments contain allusions to Psalm 69:21 and Psalm 22:18, two biblical prayers that express the agony of the believer who continues to trust in God even in the midst of pain and distress. The theme of these Psalms will be the key to Matthew's interpretation of Jesus' death.

As Jesus is pinned to the cross between two thieves, with a placard declaring the charge over his head, an amazing procession of mockery begins to file by. The taunts of the passers-by, of the Jewish leaders, and even of Jesus' fellow prisoners bring forward in ironic terms the Gospel's claims about Jesus: his authority over the Temple, his ability to save others, his claim to be the Messiah, the King of Israel, and above all, his abiding trust in his Father. That Jesus was the obedient and beloved Son of God has been the most insistent claim of Matthew's Gospel. Now in words taken from Psalm 22 (cf. Ps 22:9; words repeated in Wisdom 2:18) and in a tone that echoes Satan's temptations at the beginning of the Gospel (cf. 4:3, 6), the ultimate challenge is hurled at the dying Jesus: "He puts his trust in God; now let God rescue him if he wants him. For he did say, 'I am the Son of God'" (43).

The finale is at hand. Darkness, a biblical sign of the end of the world (cf. Am 8:9) settles over the land. Jesus' last word is said (46). He recites the opening verse of Psalm 22, a prayer of deepest agony and deepest faith. Even his prayer is mocked, as the Hebrew word *Eli* ("my God") is deliberately misunderstood as *Elijah,* the popular Old Testament figure called upon by Jews in distress, and who was expected to come before the Messiah (47). And a last act of compassion is denied Jesus (49). Finally he cries out again in prayer and obediently returns to his Father the gift of life that had been his (50; for this biblical way of describing death, cf. Gn 35:18).

Jesus' death triggers an explosion of astounding signs (51–53). The great veil before the sanctuary of the Temple is ripped in two, a quake splits the earth and breaks open the tombs of the dead, and the "holy men" rise from their tombs and prepare to enter the Holy City of Jerusalem. This cataclysmic series of events, with the exception of the tearing of the veil, is unique to Matthew's Gospel and provides the evangelist's comment on the significance of Jesus' death. These kinds of "signs" were the very events that Judaism expected to take place at the end of the world, when Yahweh would come to establish his kingdom. And this is precisely what Matthew intends to say. The tearing of the Temple veil symbolizes that the old order has passed and now a new way to God is possible through the risen Jesus. And further, Jesus' ultimate act of love and obedience has ushered in a new age. Death has been defeated, and a resurrected people march in triumph to Jerusalem. Matthew seems to allude in these verses to the haunting vision of the dry bones in the book of Ezekiel, where Yahweh breathes new life into a people without hope: "I am now going to open your graves; I mean to raise you from your graves, my people, and lead you back to the soil of Israel . . ." (Ezk 37:12).

The centurion and his soldiers add the bottom line. Seeing the effect of Jesus' death, these gentile witnesses answer the challenge of the mockers (cf. 27:43) with reverent awe: "In truth this was a Son of God" (54). Jesus' word is trustworthy. His compassion, no empty gesture. As he had pledged, he fulfilled all that was asked of him (cf. 3:15). He was indeed the beloved, obedient Son of God, and in him the will of the Father was revealed.

The death scene ends on a muted note. The faithful women who stand by the cross (55–56) and who witness the burial, signal the event that Matthew, in a sense, has already anticipated. They will be the Easter messengers who discover the empty tomb and who first meet the risen Lord (28:1–10). But opposition continues to dog Jesus even after his death. By relating the story of the guards at the tomb (27:62–66), Matthew prepares a counterattack for an alternate explanation of the empty tomb that apparently still circulated in Jewish circles contemporaneous with Matthew (cf. below 28:11–15).

STUDY QUESTION: The Gospel is not a private, personal story. Matthew insists that the implications of Jesus' death and resurrection are universal, even cosmic. Through his obedient death and the victory of his resurrection, Jesus has brought a new age of life to humanity. Does our faith stretch that far? Does it shape our view of history and of the ultimate meaning of human life?

OUT INTO A NEW WORLD:
THE RISEN LORD COMMISSIONS HIS CHURCH

¹ 28 After the sabbath, and toward dawn on the first day of the week, Mary of Magdala and ² the other Mary went to visit the sepulcher. ·And all at once there was a violent earthquake, for the angel of the Lord, descending from heaven, came ³ and rolled away the stone and sat on it. ·His face ⁴ was like lightning, his robe white as snow. ·The guards were so shaken, so frightened of him, that ⁵ they were like dead men. ·But the angel spoke; and he said to the women, "There is no need for you to be afraid. I know you are looking for ⁶ Jesus, who was crucified. ·He is not here, for he has risen, as he said he would. Come and see the ⁷ place where he lay, ·then go quickly and tell his disciples, 'He has risen from the dead and now he is going before you to Galilee; it is there you ⁸ will see him.' Now I have told you." ·Filled with awe and great joy the women came quickly away from the tomb and ran to tell the disciples.

⁹ And there, coming to meet them, was Jesus. "Greetings," he said. And the women came up to him and, falling down before him, clasped his ¹⁰ feet. ·Then Jesus said to them, "Do not be afraid; go and tell my brothers that they must leave for Galilee; they will see me there."

¹¹   While they were on their way, some of the guard went off into the city to tell the chief
¹² priests all that had happened. ·These held a meeting with the elders and, after some discussion, handed a considerable sum of money to the sol-
¹³ diers ·with these instructions, "This is what you must say, 'His disciples came during the night and
¹⁴ stole him away while we were asleep.' ·And should the governor come to hear of this, we undertake to put things right with him ourselves
¹⁵ and to see that you do not get into trouble." ·The soldiers took the money and carried out their instructions, and to this day that is the story among the Jews.
¹⁶   Meanwhile the eleven disciples set out for Galilee, to the mountain where Jesus had ar-
¹⁷ ranged to meet them. ·When they saw him they
¹⁸ fell before him, though some hesitated. ·Jesus came up and spoke to them. He said, "All authority in heaven and on earth has been given to me.
¹⁹ Go, therefore, make disciples of all the nations; baptize them in the name of the Father and of
²⁰ the Son and of the Holy Spirit, ·and teach them to observe all the commands I gave you. And know that I am with you always; yes, to the end of time."

✠

Matthew's description of the death of Jesus almost makes the Easter story anticlimactic. Signs of the resurrection break out (27:51–54) at the very moment of Jesus' obedient death. The former age, symbolized by the Temple, has passed. Because of Jesus' death, the best hopes of God's people are revived and an unlikely community of gentile soldiers acclaim Jesus as God's Son. But the Easter story is not superfluous, for it gives Matthew the chance to spell out in detail what is ex-

pected of those who live in the new age as disciples of
the risen Jesus.

The discovery of the empty tomb is quickly told
(28:1–8). As in Mark's account (cf. 16:1–8), the
women return to the tomb on Sunday. An incredible
discovery awaits them. Matthew's version heightens the
glory of this moment by adding the details about the
earthquake, a resplendent "angel of the Lord," the
rolling back of the rock, and the terror of the soldiers
(2–4). These things, too, characterized Jewish expectations about the kind of events that would come at the
end of the world. Matthew, then, continues to remind
his readers that with the death and resurrection of
Jesus a new and final age of history has begun.

The angel interprets the meaning of the empty tomb
(an interpretation whose origin and substance are
meant to stand in sharp contrast to the fabrication
drawn up in 28:11–15). The Jesus who was crucified
is not to be found among the dead. He is risen, just as
he had promised. As in almost all the Gospel resurrection stories, those who are privileged witnesses are
given a "mission." The women are to alert the scattered disciples that Jesus will gather them together in
Galilee. The women leave the tomb charged with "awe
and great joy."

That joy is compounded as they meet the risen Lord
himself (9–10). It is really Jesus who has risen; they
are able to touch his feet. But he is also clearly the
risen Lord, and so they fall down in worship. The mission given by the angel is reiterated. They are to tell
Jesus' "brothers" to meet him in Galilee. "Brothers" is
the very title of solidarity that Jesus had used in urging
unlimited forgiveness and reconciliation among those
who would enter the kingdom (cf. 18:19–20, 35).

Matthew's closing scene (28:16–20) weaves together into a breath-taking tapestry the brilliant threads that have run throughout his Gospel. Jesus, who had climbed a hill to proclaim words of grace and compassion to a sick humanity (Chs. 5–7), Jesus, who on another mountain had blinded his disciples with a glimpse of his future glory (Ch. 17), now stands in majesty on a summit in Galilee. This Jesus, whose roots reach back to Abraham and David, whose words and works have identified him as the Christ, as God's own Servant and Son, is now clearly recognized as the victorious Son of Man, that mysterious figure whom Daniel had prophesied would bear "all authority on heaven and on earth" (Dn 7:14). This same Jesus moves forward to heal and transform the "eleven disciples," whose number testifies to the wounds of betrayal, of fear, of "little faith," of doubt (17). But these "little ones" will be the very ones to proclaim the gospel and to build the community of the New Age. Their mission is no longer confined to Israel (cf. 10:5) but must be to "all nations." They are to make disciples, to baptize, and to teach. The "law" of this new people is to be the law that has fulfilled the old Law of Moses: Jesus' own teaching. Fidelity to that command of love would be the branding mark of those called into the kingdom.

To begin his Gospel, Matthew had borrowed from the First Book of Chronicles, whose panoramic history of the Jewish kings had attempted to give Israel perspective in a time of confusion and discontinuity. Matthew seems to turn to this book again in shaping the conclusion of his Gospel. The final chapter of the Second Book of Chronicles ends with a solemn decree of Cyrus, king of Persia. This unexpected instrument of God's providence had released the people of Israel from their exile and commanded them to build a new people and a new Temple.

Now, centuries later, God's providence once again reaches out to bring his people back to life. But, this time, the herald of the good news is no Persian king but God's own Son, One whose infinite grace and startling power are revealed in the name he bears: Emmanuel, "God-with-us." The revelation of this name stood at the beginning of Matthew's gospel story (1:23). The promise of abiding presence which that same name inspires concludes the story: "And know that I am with you always; yes, to the end of time."

STUDY QUESTION: Matthew's Gospel gives the church a breath-taking commission: to be a resurrection people, full of life and faith; to be a community founded in Christ's name and obedient to his command of love; to be believable witnesses of the presence of the risen Lord in his world. The question lingers: are we that people of the new age?

SUGGESTED FURTHER READINGS

W. D. Davies. *The Sermon on the Mount.* New York: Cambridge University Press, 1966. Paper. An abridgment of a larger work by this author that offers a detailed study of the sermon and its background in Judaism and early Christianity.

P. F. Ellis. *Matthew: His Mind and His Message.* Collegeville, Minn.: The Liturgical Press, 1974. Paper. A study of the structure and theology of Matthew.

J. C. Fenton. *Saint Matthew.* Pelican Gospel Commentaries. Baltimore: Penguin Books, 1963. Paper.

H. B. Green. *The Gospel According to Matthew.* New Clarendon Bible. London: Oxford University Press, 1975. A very concise, moderately technical commentary.

J. D. Kingsbury. *Matthew: Structure, Christology, Kingdom.* Philadelphia: Fortress Press, 1975. The title reveals the contents of this thorough study of key theological concepts in Matthew.

E. Schweizer. *The Good News According to Matthew.* Atlanta: John Knox Press, 1975. One of the most extensive modern commentaries on Matthew now in English.

D. Senior. "The Ministry of Continuity: Matthew's Gospel and the Interpretation of History," *The Bible Today* 82 (1976), 629–708. This article lays out in more detail the theological purpose of Matthew described in the Introduction.

———. *Matthew: A Gospel for the Church.* Herald Biblical Booklets. Chicago: Franciscan Herald Press, 1973. Paper. A study of the structure and theology of Matthew, designed for the non-professional reader.

H. C. Waetjen. *The Origin and Destiny of Humanness.* Corte Madera, Calif.: Omega Books, 1976. Paper. The author traces the theological conception of Matthew as it unfolds in the structure and style of his Gospel.